D0442028

# Developing Understanding in
# Primary Mathematics

# Developing Understanding in Primary Mathematics: Key Stages 1 and 2

*Edited by*

Andrew Davis

*and*

Deirdre Pettitt

 The Falmer Press

(A member of the Taylor & Francis Group)
London • Washington, D.C.

**UK**     The Falmer Press, 4 John Street, London WC1N 2ET
**USA**    The Falmer Press, Taylor & Francis Inc., 1900 Frost Road, Suite 101, Bristol, PA 19007

---

© A. Davis and D. Pettitt 1994

*All rights reserved. No part of this publication may be reproduced, stored in a retrieval system, or transmitted in any form or by any means, electronic, mechanical, photocopying, recording or otherwise, without permission in writing from the Publisher.*

First published in 1994

**A catalogue record for this book is available from the British Library**

**Library of Congress Cataloging-in-Publication Data are available on request**

ISBN 0 7507 0357 1 cased
ISBN 0 7507 0358 X paper

Jacket design by Caroline Archer

Typeset in 11/13 pt Garamond by
Graphicraft Typesetters Ltd., Hong Kong.

*Printed in Great Britain by Burgess Science Press, Basingstoke on paper which has a specified pH value on final paper manufacture of not less than 7.5 and is therefore 'acid free'.*

# Contents

# 1    Introduction

*Andrew Davis*

'What is the capital of France, Smith?'

'Er . . . Madrid, sir.'

'No, Smith. Stand up! Paris is the capital city of France. What is the capital of France, Davis?'

I had a copy of '*The Hobbit*' on my knees. I was making furtive efforts to read it, raising my head every so often to masquerade as an attentive pupil.

'Edinburgh, sir.'

'STAND UP, DAVIS!'

The book slid to the floor with a crash, observed grimly by the teacher.

'What is the capital of France, Fisher?'

'Paris, sir.'

'Thank you, Fisher.'

The teacher slowly approached my desk. I knew what would happen next. . . .

Such scenes were a dreary and frequent part of my childhood at primary school. In the nineteen nineties, it would be difficult to discover living examples of this teaching style. Yet its model of learning still persists. Many people, including some politicians think that learning is a kind of copying. There are items to be copied; 'facts' about number, or historical events, or gravity, for instance. The learner takes a copy of these facts into her head. She can then easily demonstrate her learning; on request, she can say or write it. Teachers in this account are thought to 'transmit' that which is to be learned: to perform the necessary actions for the pupil to acquire a copy of the teacher's version of the facts.

What might these 'necessary actions' be? On the face of it, standing up at the front and simply 'telling' should be quite sufficient. Teachers stuff the rucksack (the pupil mind) with contents (facts) or perhaps pour knowledge into children (who start off empty). Shuard remarked in a famous broadcast that pupils had proved to be very leaky vessels.

In effect learning *per se* is being equated with one of its particular varieties, namely rote learning (Bailey, 1984). Now arguably it is a pity that we no longer ask children to memorize poems or historical dates. Most teachers have always expected children to learn number bonds and tables; their expectations have now been backed up by National Curriculum requirements. However, the bulk of primary mathematics should not only be taken into the memory but also digested thoroughly. Information which is merely memorized cannot be used or applied in the everyday world, for it can be 'in' the mind without being understood.

Rote learning is a relatively simple phenomenon to grasp. Other varieties of learning, where the 'digesting' is more comprehensive, are in many ways deeply mysterious. It is much easier to attack incorrect accounts than to tell a positive story. This book tries to rise to such a positive challenge, for Key Stages 1 and 2 mathematics in particular. The next chapter makes some general observations about mathematics learning, subsequently developed and applied in practical ways.

The 'transmission' model of teaching, we will contend, fails to take account of the nature of much mathematical knowledge and understanding, and of the clear implications for the ways in which mathematics must be learned. How then should we help children to develop mathematical understanding? What are the appropriate roles for the teacher?

We argue that certain kinds of classroom contexts together with particular teaching styles, are especially likely to stimulate pupils to 'construct' or 'invent' their own mathematical understanding. A selection of these ideas for classroom application are discussed in detail. The latter constitute the heart of this book. To attack transmission theories of learning is scarcely original and we devote only a section of the second chapter to doing so. Nevertheless, we are conscious that criticism of such theory has had frustratingly little effect on educational policy or classroom practice in the last fifteen years; hence we do not apologize too abjectly for raising objections in print yet again.[1]

Our experience tells us that some primary teachers agree with our approach. Those who do and who enjoy labels could say they were 'constructivist' in outlook and that they believed in 'constructivism'. We make much use of this term. A well-thought out constructivism can be a valuable acquisition for teachers whose convictions were previously at the tacit intuitive level. Views of teaching and learning held by politically influential groups are in stark contrast to constructivism, and in such a climate it is especially important to be able to support practice with a coherent and readily justifiable theoretical position.

Transmission culture was thought to be very much in retreat in the fifties and sixties. It is often claimed that the scene was dominated then by child-centred ideas. Child-centredness meant different things to different people. It referred to styles of teaching, to a set of moral attitudes to children and in particular to the view that pupils should exercise substantial control over their own learning. Confusion abounded, but lurking behind some of the opposition to the then prevailing fashion for formal whole class teaching was an intuitive rejection of transmission as a model of teaching and learning. However, even that rejection itself was confused with a superficial hostility to teachers talking to large groups of children. We will see later that a constructivist teacher may well choose at times to work directly with the whole class.

Many of us now know that child-centred thinking in whatever guise actually made only a modest impact on the practice of most primary schools. Transmission remained a potent model for learning at the classroom level. Whole class teaching, with which transmission was and still is confused became politically incorrect on some initial teacher education courses and in some LEAs (Alexander, 1992). For the last fifteen years or so transmission has once more become politically correct in the context of national education policy.

Chapter 2 outlines a version of constructivism which underlies the rest of the book. Constructivism is quite fashionable at present among theorists, much of it vague or incoherent. Our objectives are not primarily academic or scholarly, and we have therefore refrained from treating critically and in detail the substantial 'constructivist' writings in the literature. To explore the exotic landscapes of von Glasersfeld and his ilk would be of little help to those closer to classroom practice, and for whom this book is written. We hope to offer a straightforward and robust version of constructivism, with clearly specifiable implications for classroom mathematics.

Chapter 3 proceeds to examine ways in which story making, narrative and drama can contribute to the growth of children's mathematical understanding. The role of the teacher is a key issue, and this is explored in detail through many examples.

The discussion then touches on the state of health of teachers' own mathematics. Adults, it is suggested, might profitably experience constructing or reconstructing aspects of their own knowledge of mathematics, thereby improving their flexibility, confidence, and capacities to help children to learn. This thought is examined with the help of some examples in chapter 4.

In chapter 5 some links between investigation, the search for pattern and constructing mathematical understanding are explored. Within investigative contexts, children can be helped to search for patterns, and enabled to discern similarities, differences, repetitions, and regularities given appropriate interactions with teachers.

Games have long been advocated as valuable aids in primary mathematics; chapter 6 illustrates ways in which games could aid children's mathematical construction. It is argued that it is the package of *games plus teachers playing certain roles* which provides the key to effective learning here.

Children may be helped in their mathematical invention through engaging in practical activities using sounds, and the next chapter illustrates ways in which this might be done. There is little which is intrinsically 'constructivist' about sounds and so much discussion is devoted to the kinds of interactions between teachers and children in these contexts which should provide good catalysts for mathematical invention.

Chapter 8 looks at young children's drawing behaviour and focuses on the surprisingly rich mathematical aspects which are developed through this. It is argued that a deeper understanding of children's drawing systems will enable teachers to heighten their own understanding of art and mathematics and therefore to be able to improve the quality of their work with children.

Children's experiences outside school play a substantial role in fostering their individual creation of mathematical structures; this affects the level of mathematical knowledge possessed by the new Reception pupil and continues to influence developments in their mathematical understanding while they are at school. Important questions arise concerning the relative contribution of school and the 'real world' to the growth of mathematical understanding. These issues are examined in the final chapter. Moreover we ask about the senses in which mathematics should be 'real' to young learners, and about the extent to which this can actually be the case. The last words in the book are left to a class teacher who might not call herself a constructivist but who has reflected long and hard on the challenges presented by teaching mathematics in the primary school. Her insights are sampled to provide a concluding commentary.

## Note

1 Child-centred thinkers in the fifties and sixties effectively criticized 'Gradgrind' teaching (a familiar reference to the Dickensian character who was obsessed with the attempt to transmit facts to his pupils). The objection was not, or should not have been to facts as such, but to Gradgrind's vision of the nature of facts and of how they might be suitably acquired.

# 2　Constructivism

*Andrew Davis*

## Introduction

In chapter 1 we met an old enemy: the 'transmission' view of learning. We regard this particular model as committing three major categories of mistake (among others).

(1)  It is wrong about the knowledge which is to be gained by pupils.
(2)  It fails to understand pupils' minds and the way they must 'store' what they learn.
(3)  The idea of transmission itself cannot properly capture how pupils learn from teachers or indeed from anyone.

In this chapter we cast light on these three interconnected mistakes as we focus on the true nature of mathematical knowledge. We will see that a proper understanding of this has clear implications for the ways in which mathematics may be effectively taught. We look at these implications in general terms in this chapter, while reserving detailed discussion of their classroom application for later.

## What is Mathematics?

It is less controversial than in the sixties to insist that a necessary condition for effective teaching is the teacher's adequate grasp of the subject. (But it is not sufficient; sadly pupils have sometimes gained little mathematics even after spending long periods with very competent mathematicians.) Furthermore, what teachers take a subject to be significantly influences how they teach it.

For example, if history for you consisted of a collection of discrete 'facts' which would include dates and statutes together with the definitive account of the 'causes of important events' you might well deem exposition to be your single most effective teaching style. Admittedly the history-as-facts model does not make such a decision inevitable. Neither however does it encourage alternatives. For instance, why on such a model bother to provide opportunities for groups of children to examine evidence and create interpretations? At the end of the day effective teaching would presumably be ensuring that individual pupils had acquired the relevant facts. Investigating, discussing, and interpreting would seem unlikely to promote this efficiently.

Suppose, on the other hand, the subject is seen as a collective understanding of 'stories' about the past. 'Doing history' would include attempts to create and grasp such narratives in the light of the evidence. According to this perspective pupils could not be treated as 'rucksacks' for historical facts; instead they would require guidance in the processes of entering into these stories; in developing for themselves appropriate narrative explanations of past events while taking account of relevant evidence.

This is but one vivid example of the links between favoured methods for teaching a given subject and views about its nature. Of course, the character of history itself is controversial. Vast passions were expended on drafts of the National Curriculum for history. The subject is inherently political and ideological; differing sets of values and visions of society are linked to particular 'stories' about past events. If history students are allowed a measure of autonomy, then there is a risk that they may come up with 'stories' which conflict with those preferred by certain political groupings.

In sharp contrast, mathematics is viewed as 'absolute', as outside political preferences (and for most, pretty uninteresting). The minor ripples around the time of the publication of the interim report of the mathematics National Curriculum working group and the resignation of a right-wing Professor of Economics, cannot hold a candle to the heady events preceding the official history ring-binder. We can imagine much more readily that teachers carry around with them differing understandings of history than that they might possess distinctive conceptions of mathematics.

Indeed, the very idea that there might be more than one view about the essence of mathematics itself may seem eccentric. Surely, it may be argued, there is no room for dispute. Its essential features are quite obvious. There are mathematical facts to be understood and learned, for example, that $2 + 2 = 4$ or that regular hexagons can be used to cover a space without gaps whereas regular pentagons cannot. There are also skills to be acquired such as those of using a compass or protractor. The facts are immutable, and, so to speak, 'out there'; they are part of the reality with which children gradually come to terms as they gain experience and education.

Some traditionalists place greater emphasis on the 'basics' of number, and could wish that primary schools spent less time on 'trendy' topics such as shape and probability. To that extent there is disagreement, but the dispute is about curriculum content, rather than the status of mathematics itself.

However, I think that we need to ponder more deeply on the nature and status of mathematics. Once we do, possibilities of alternative and indeed rival conceptions begin to emerge. Let us begin with the thought that mathematics is somehow 'out there', independently of us. There is an insidious mixture of truth and falsity in this vague and rather philosophical-sounding idea. The false elements in the mixture can distort our thinking about mathematics learning.

It IS true in some sense that, for instance, $2 + 2 = 4$, whether I think so or not. I recall an argument with my father when I was a boy; in a spirit of mischief I denied that God could contrive that 2 and 2 were 5. My father, concerned that I was setting limits on God's power, asserted that He jolly well could. My father was wrong, I was right, but no doubt at the wrong time and in the wrong way as usual. I was not undermining divine omnipotence since, given the way we use the terms, $2 + 2 = 5$ does not make sense. There isn't anything which God can't perform here; we have said nothing to His discredit — any more than if we denied that He could come up with a square circle, a married bachelor or a biped with seven legs.

We emphasized 'given the way we use the terms'. This draws attention to the damaging falsity which may lurk in some assertions of the objective and independent character of mathematics. Such contentions misleadingly distance mathematics from human activities. In actual fact it is people who create and operate rules for the use of mathematical terms and symbols. Needless to say this does not happen in the course of one generation. This has been going on since the dawn of history. Anyhow $2 + 2 = 4$ has the meaning that it does, partly in virtue of our agreement about how to use '2', '4', '=' and '+'. We invent or construct mathematics; it is a human product. Once thought through and expressed, however, its truths are not subject to arbitrary and individual whim. Given our agreed use of relevant symbols, then, as we noted above, '$2 + 2 = 4$' conveys a truth whether I think so or not.

Speaking of children 'constructing' or 'inventing' mathematics does not imply that next year's Y2 pupils at my local infant school might come up with a 'new' arithmetic. They might agree to a deviant use of the symbol '4', so that it meant 5. But this would be pretty silly, and it would not mean that in the orthodox sense that 2 and 2 did not make 4. It would imply rather that our tiresomely imaginative infants could not use the number sentence '2 + 2 = 4' to state what we mean when we say that 2 and 2 are 4, and hence would have to have another way of stating that particular truth.

It must be conceded that this claimed combination of human invention and objectivity can seem so puzzling as to verge on the paradoxical. We might instead be tempted to join Plato in thinking of mathematicians as journeying in thought within some unearthly abstract realm and making discoveries there, communicating them on occasion to lesser mortals. However, this temptation should be resisted.

Paul Ernest conveniently summarizes the human invention view of mathematics; he terms it 'social constructivism':

> ... objective knowledge of mathematics is social, and is not contained in texts or other recorded materials, nor in some ideal realm. Objective knowledge of mathematics resides in the shared rules, conventions, understandings and meanings of the individual members of society, and in their interactions (and consequently, their social institutions) (Ernest, P., 1991).

### Mathematical Facts

It might seem that we can easily get hold of mathematical facts. We could begin to 'list them, filling many pages with statements about numbers, space and shape. However, it is important to appreciate fully that in doing this we have not actually 'got hold' of individual items in any sense. Mathematical facts and concepts do not, and cannot 'exist' on their own, in splendid isolation. They are embedded within complex clusters of others.

For example, consider 2. Certainly 2 refers to that which all sets with 2 members have in common. But it is a great deal more — 2 has a *position* in the number system. It relates to 3, 4, 5, 1, 0, etc.; it has an ordinal value. The richer the account we provide for 2, the more we must spell out these connections and relationships. There is no complete story. The same point holds good of number sentences in which 2 occurs, even of the simple '2 + 3 = 5' variety. The very identity of the fact that 2 + 3 = 5 is bound up with its relationship with other number facts. Any attempt to explain it has to appeal to the structure of the number system, the conventional rules for '+' and '=' and much else.

## The Implications of this for Learning

So mathematics is not a fixed inhuman abstract system which we discover. On the contrary it is created by us, our forbears and our descendants; as learners we are continually inventing and reinventing it. And what we create is a system of interlocking concepts and rules as opposed to a series of discrete facts. It is this system that pupils must learn. They cannot and need not commit to memory a comprehensive list of mathematical statements conveying the facts. There would be too many, indeed the list could never be completed!

(They should, of course memorize basic number bonds and multiplication tables. Such memorizing can be very effective and efficient but clearly it needs to be highly selective. It is pointless unless the pupil *already* understands that which she is now arranging in her mind for instant access. Good teachers give considerable thought to the best time in the pupil's development for such memorizing to be encouraged.)

So, the child digesting mathematics will need gradually to acquire ownership of complex networks of concepts, symbols and terms. However, she does not come to school in a state of ignorance. Already present in her mind are emergent and probably to a degree erroneous complexes of mathematical concepts. Her mathematics will have much in common with that of her friends, but it is also likely to be individual and idiosyncratic to some degree.

Fresh mathematics must be absorbed by the child's resident mental networks. Otherwise it is taken into the mind, if at all, on a rote basis. It is not understood, and cannot inform the child's future speech and behaviour except by being quotable on demand. Even as this absorption occurs, the new learning transforms the existing networks, sometimes trivially, and at other times radically. Some may recall Piaget's ideas in this regard. He spoke of the processes of making 'new' knowledge fit into existing structures as assimilation, and the modification of those structures to cope with the fresh knowledge as accommodation, though in no real sense are there 'two' processes. Piaget may rather be seen as drawing our attention to two fundamental aspects of the learning process.

Consider Parveen, who has a good understanding of numbers to 100. She has long appreciated their function for basic counting. She comprehends their interrelationships — that 12 is 2 more than 10 and hence that 10 is 2 less than 12, and realizes something of the significance of the digits in several digit numbers — that is, she is beginning to achieve some grasp of place value. She is provided by her teacher with a programme of activities about fractions. She learns about dividing wholes into equal parts (the 'cake model' of fractions), and about dividing sets or groups into equal subsets to find fractions of them — splitting 12 into 2 equal parts to find what half of 12 amounts to, and so forth. One day she encounters the idea that fractions have a place on the number line. Fractions themselves are numbers which come between the whole numbers. To absorb this astounding thought, she must change her existing grasp of numbers as a system to count with. Ripples from the new idea travel through her resident network of number concepts, and subtle transformations occur. Numbers are no longer merely devices for counting. They can pinpoint a quantity. There can be nearly two metres of wool. There are any number of numbers between the whole numbers. She can begin to make sense of answers to calculations, such as 5 divided by 3.

New mathematical facts cannot be taken in to a child's head 'one at a time' since, as we have seen, a single fact considered alone has virtually no meaning or identity. (In rote learning a child might be thought to acquire a single 'fact'. Yet all that need actually happen in pure rote learning is that the child can acquire the capacity to produce a sentence of some kind, regardless of its meaning. So there is no significant sense in which the child is gaining knowledge at all.)

It follows that the pupil cannot receive a straight copy of a fact possessed by her teacher. Whatever is 'gained' during a successful lesson cannot be picked out in any simplistic fashion. Further, in today's activity Jane may well receive something very different from Philip, since the mathematics in her mind at the beginning of the lesson will almost certainly differ from his in quantity, structure and quality (Davis, 1993; Davis, 1990).

## What is it to Know Something Mathematical?

The assault on a transmission model of teaching may be redoubled by considering more directly what it is to know something mathematical. This is best tackled through a mundane example.

What is it to know that $15 + 14 = 29$? As we have already said, we are discussing knowledge with a measure of understanding as opposed to memorizing only. Let us not even attempt to specify how much understanding we have in mind, but just make it clear that we are assuming some. It would in fact be impossible to list all the possible ways in which a child might show that she had this knowledge, but we can make a workmanlike beginning.

For example, a child can certainly respond with the answer '29' when asked what 14 and 15 are altogether, and would cope with a range of terminology in which this same question might be couched. She will appreciate that giving 14 smarties to Jane who already has 15 will mean Jane ends up with 29, that when she buys a pencil for 14p and a rubber for 15p she will spend 29p altogether, that her sister who is 14 will be 29 in 15 years time, and so on.

In effect, we have outlined a requirement that the child possesses a relational as opposed to an instrumental understanding (Skemp, R., 1989). Skemp asks us to imagine that two people, say Smith and Jones, are trying to find their way from A to B in a strange town. Smith has directions such as 'Take the first right . . . under the railway bridge, then the second left . . . past the church, then right again.' Jones has similar instructions, but in addition has a map, and can find A on it. If Smith follows the directions precisely, with no mistakes, he will reach B. With a single error, he may well become totally lost. If Jones fails to follow the directions properly, he can use the map to find his way back into the sequence of instructions. Or he can even devise another route altogether. During his explorations he may even be able to extend the map!

Smith resembles a pupil with instrumental understanding. She may know some procedures to obtain the right answer. In the case of 15 + 14 she may realize that if she writes the 14 under the 15, adds the right hand digits for each number and puts the total underneath, adds the left hand digits and puts that total, then the teacher will tick her answer. She perhaps has no idea of the magnitude of the answer to expect from this calculation. She may not grasp which number is represented by the digits '2' and '9' in her answer. She might even be hazy about which number '15' represents, and fail to appreciate that it is between 10 and 20. If, given the calculation 15 + 16, she might rigidly apply the same algorithm, end up with the answer 211, and have no notion that any-thing has gone wrong.

In a caricature of the Suzuki method for teaching violin, it may be claimed that it enables *anyone* to learn the instrument, regardless of what is taking place or even what *could* take place in that person's head. Our pupil with instrumental understanding alone might be dubbed a Suzuki mathematician.

Jones, on the other hand, models a pupil with relational under-standing. She might use the algorithm for adding several-digit numbers, but has other methods up her sleeve. She would know before she started that the answer would be around 30. If anything went wrong, she could effect a 'repair' to her faulty procedure because she knows what she is about. She has a comprehensive 'map' in her head of numbers, operations and their interrelationships. If she becomes lost, she can find her way back.

Children require rich cognitive maps of the mathematics with which they are working if they are to achieve a good relational understanding of it. And for the child to be capable of the almost infinite variety of possible manifestations of the knowledge that 15 + 14 = 29, she must possess relational rather than instrumental understanding. To speak of 'cognitive maps' is to invest heavily in metaphor whose full implications are not easy to specify. With this caution in mind, we may suggest tentatively that levels of relational understanding seem in part to be tied to the degree to which the essential interconnectedness of mathematical concepts is mirrored satisfactorily in the mind of the child. She must also link her networks of mathematical concepts to a wealth of everyday notions so that she can just as easily cope with adding children, money or sweets as apply numbers to cars in the car park or houses on the street.

It should be very clear from the foregoing that a pupil could not simply take a discrete item (a fact) from the teacher as a naive transmission model appears to imply. Teachers must rather search for activities which seem likely to enhance the 'interconnectedness' of learners' knowledge, and to facilitate the development within each child of their personal and idiosyncratic networks of concepts. Much of this book is designed to support such a search.

## Constructivism and the Control of Learning

Having discussed objections to the transmission model of learning in particular, we proceed to make some further general observations about our constructivism. While its language may be unfamiliar to some, there are many for whom the apparent emphasis on learning rather than teaching will have Piagetian echoes. Constructivism in the broadest sense owes fundamental intellectual debts to Piaget. Yet this association also has its disadvantages. A great deal of Piagetian baggage must be discarded in our search for a defensible constructivism.

The constructivist might, for instance be Piagetian enough to say that he focuses on learning rather than teaching. This would be an error of judgment. It would allow the term 'teaching' to be hijacked and to be reserved for teacher activities 'from the front', where 'telling' children dominates the scene.

In protest at this attempt at verbal piracy, it must be asserted that a great variety of actions, processes and styles may appropriately be characterized as teaching. Explanation and exposition have their place, and may have been neglected in recent decades. Yet we also need to consider listening, discussing, questioning, hypothesizing, inviting pupils to hypothesize or speculate, demonstrating, acting as a reference book, refusing to answer, joining in children's play and many other forms of behaviour. All these could be teaching. Once this is realized, we can briskly deny that our constructivism is focusing on learning rather than teaching. It has major implications for both.

A group of five-year-olds are playing with Duplo. Plastic people smile from the doors of their plastic houses. A lorry carries 'bottles of milk' to the houses.

'How many bottles does the lady in the blue house want today?' inquires the teacher.

'Two,' responds a child.

'You'd better leave a message for the milkman then.'

The child obtains a piece of card and a felt tip pen, and proceeds to draw two bottles on it. The card is then deposited on the 'doorstep'. The rest of the group join in with enthusiasm.

Without too much in the way of heavy pressure, the teacher succeeds in acquiring the role of milkman after the game has been under way for a few minutes. Where a child has asked for one pint of milk, the teacher leaves two. A message for two pints elicits a response of three.

'This milkman is silly,' a child announces, with some enjoyment.

'I bet you can't make the silly milkman give you the milk you really want,' remarks the teacher provocatively.

Some of the children ignore this. Steven, however is intrigued. He ponders the problem for a moment, and then grins privately to himself. He puts out a message for one pint. The milkman leaves two.

'Ha! Ha! Caught you, silly milkman. I wanted two pints. That's why I said one pint!'

There is now a clamour to be allowed to be the silly milkman. The teacher, with some uneasiness at exercising this degree of control, relinquishes her role only on condition that the next milkman does not simply mimic her silliness, but must decide on a new way of being silly. After some false starts in which the rules are changed each time instead of a new pattern of deviance being allowed to settle down, the milk-man learns to keep to a rule of leaving two pints too many.

Later, after the teacher has been away from the game for some time, there are difficulties because Steven has gone for the rule of 'one too few', and Anna puts out the agreed message for 'no pints today please' (the message for indicating zero itself having given rise to much heated argument). The teacher returns to quell the acrimony; she cannot make any suggestion to solve the problem and neither can the children. That is a risk when children take charge of games and the mathematics that may be part of them.

This is but one instance of a type of activity we will be saying a good deal more about in the next chapter. It shows the location of control over key aspects of a mathematics task moving away from the teacher to the pupil. Pupils may from time to time begin to make decisions about who they work with. They may select which materials to use, and how long to carry on with a particular task. They may, either alone or in groups, set up new problems and proceed to solve them.

No one is suggesting that it is wrong for teachers to exercise substantial control over children's learning. It may well be highly appropriate on many occasions. So what is the justification for relinquishing selected aspects of control in some lessons?

The beginnings of one possible answer is as follows. We have just noted that children differ one from another in respect of their current mathematical attainment, often in extremely complex ways not readily identifiable by the most perceptive teacher. While children will not always know which piece of learning they can best tackle next, they necessarily have a form of privileged awareness of their own understanding levels and of their associated feelings. They may not be able to tell their teachers directly about all this. Admittedly self-inspection need not provide infallible insights. Yet children could still make decisions to some extent based on such self-awareness if given the opportunity. Why not then sometimes provide them with scope to decide for themselves how and at what level to tackle problems? Their choices may well turn out to be soundly based on knowledge about their own conceptual mastery, knowledge wholly or partially unavailable to their teacher.

The 'silly milkman' play activity shows a teacher teaching, but in a variety of guises, none of them having much to do with 'delivering'. It demonstrates the risks that activities will develop in directions not amenable to carefully pre-specified mathematical objectives; abandoning teaching as 'transmission' means setting aside that control opportunity. During their play, pupils initiate ideas in which they have confidence; the level of their thinking should closely relate to their own mathematical competence in this relaxed and open context.

Recent publications from NCC and SEAC have made familiar the distinction between 'differentiation by task' and 'differentiation by outcome'. In the former approach the teacher sets tasks according to the pupils' level of knowledge, understanding and skills. In the latter approach the teacher offers a more 'open' activity, with a degree of control passed to the pupils, who work at a range of levels depending on their current attainments. It is commonplace (but not necessarily unproblematic) in language, art and drama, for instance, to opt for differentiation by outcome; frequently where children are asked to write a story the whole class is given the same stimulus. The standard of the resulting written products ranges widely. Equally widespread is the practice in maths of (apparently) opting for a rigid differentiation by task; children work on individual paths through maths schemes according to their current attainments. (However, it is well-known that this is in fact only an illusion of differentiation by task. Children can reach advanced books in a scheme while having very little idea of the mathematics involved, which means that tasks are not being set them according to their current attainment. We cannot pursue that point further here.)

If the constructivist applications in later chapters are implemented, there will be a fairly dramatic change in mathematics teaching styles, with much more differentiation by outcome. There will be many occasions on which pupils take a considerable degree of responsibility for the pace and level of their own mathematical learning. This is not to imply that differentiation by task in mathematics is 'wrong'. It is rather to claim that a one-sided diet of such differentiation is inappropriate.

Some will recall the example given in the Non-Statutory Guidance in the first version of the National Curriculum, where a closed task is instanced as $3 \times 5 = ?$, while the suggested corresponding 'open' task is: 'Make up some questions whose answer is 15'. The first style exemplifies differentiation by task, whereas the second, at least to some degree, permits differentiation by outcome. It is easy to see how the second task requires and is likely to develop relational understanding, whereas the first neither requires nor is particularly likely to develop such understanding.

Clearly the demands made on the teacher where pupils are following open tasks become more varied, challenging and subtle than those envisaged in a transmission model. If only it were possible simply to transmit to children their mathematics, to pour the subject into their heads! Life would be much easier. At the same time, the teacher's task would be much less challenging and exciting.

## Constructivism: Other Points

From Piaget we also inherit the contention that children must be active creators of their own mental structures; the more abstract thought of which older children and adults are capable is internalized action. In a hazy way this may seem to imply that children should be 'busy' in practical ways in the classroom; that they should constantly be doing maths with materials, and preferably should be physically active at least some of the time. Again, the version of constructivism defended in this book does not share this contention. The criteria for being 'active' would be difficult to explain, since the idea is inherently vague. Many of the contexts for construction suggested in the book do involve 'active' pupils. But there is no reason why children should not at times be sitting quietly listening to the teacher explaining something. The crucial point is to note what should be going on 'in their heads' if the teaching is effective. Pupils will not be taking on board 'copies' of something in the teacher's possession. They will rather be making links between what they already know and understand, and the material being explained to them. Often they *are* forming relevant connections when active, but if Piagetian theory implies that they cannot do this when sitting still, then so much the worse for Piagetian theory.

Another point about teaching styles which apparently stemmed from perceived Piagetian orthodoxies: the idea of waiting until children are 'ready', and then providing them with a stimulating environment so that their mental structures more or less spontaneously develop to the next 'level', is generally attributed to Piaget. Regardless of whether such attribution is fair, our constructivism certainly does not suggest any such '*laissez-faire*' or 'educational impresario' approach by the teacher. In contrast, we have many detailed thoughts to offer about direct teacher interventions.

We make the assumption throughout this book that to encourage interactive working and discussions of certain kinds is likely to foster the growth of a greater number and range of connections between mathematical elements than an unrelieved diet of solitary study. The complex process of developing adequate cognitive maps of the relevant mathematics can be greatly enhanced through appropriate social interaction in which, of course, language will play a key role.

Mathematical activities which are 'social' can reflect the social aspects of mathematical meanings. In the 'silly milkman' scenario, children in effect agree to play by given rules of counting and on how to apply these rules, given particular messages left for the milkman by the householders.

To Vygotsky we are indebted for the thought that children talking with their teachers in meaningful practical situations can develop or construct 'new' mathematical understanding which at that point in their development would be impossible without the teacher. This thought needs extending, however. Children *interacting* in the presence of a skilled teacher can be enabled to develop their mathematical thinking *within their group* in ways which would be impossible without the teacher. It probably requires the presence of the teacher, for instance, for new rules for errant counting to be maintained for any length of time in the silly milkman activity. Later chapters suggest many contexts in which such teacher supported group interactions might readily and effectively take place.

## Conclusion: Isn't all this just Common Sense?

One reaction from even the sympathetic reader may be that all this is just 'too true to be good'. Everyone with any sense agrees with it; there are simply enormous practical problems about applying it in the classroom. Or, to look at it another way, perhaps it *is* being applied now, since we allowed above that children might even be quietly in their seats listening to the teacher and still be playing roles as constructivist learners. Perhaps every teacher is a constructivist, whether they would admit it or not. In fact, it begins to look as if nothing could count as *not* being a constructivist. Any imaginable teaching style can be seen as manifesting constructivism! Constructivism is an empty theory since it cannot be falsified.

In response, it has to be conceded that once you abandon the exotic intellectual avenues, many of which currently attract the 'constructivist' label, you are certainly closer to common sense, valued by all primary teachers. And we are not advancing here a constructivist theory of learning as a rival to other theories of learning. Our constructivism is not an account of what we discovered through experience and/or from the insights of scientists about how and why children learn mathematics most effectively. Perhaps 'theory' is not an appropriate word to use of our constructivism at all. In our hands it chiefly concerns a fairly mundane appreciation of what it is to know and understand something in mathematics, or indeed more generally; it is the insight that this appreciation clashes with the transmission model of learning, still favoured by influential groups in our society.

There is a little more to it, however, than common sense. 'Social constructivism' as an account of mathematics itself and as characterized by Paul Ernest, represents something of a departure from 'common sense'. At least, this is so if the intuitive common sense view of mathematics is that of Plato — as an abstract indestructible structure which exists independently of human activity. And it is the 'social' in 'social constructivism' which we use to support our later emphasis on children working in groups with the teacher, thinking explicitly about rules and procedures for operating within mathematics.

Finally, by way of riposte to our imaginary objector here, there is all the difference between a class of engaged learners listening to a teacher, and a class of passive recipients in the presence of a teacher who is convinced that transmission of mathematical understanding is possible. This is obvious, even if superficially each classroom event might be put into the same category of teaching style.

# 3 Using Story and Drama to Develop Mathematics

*Andrew Davis, Peter Millward and Deirdre Pettitt*

## Introduction

Few familiar with young children can doubt the extraordinary motivating power of two connected themes: story and 'socio-dramatic play'. School yards used to ring with the sound of 'cops and robbers'; now it is more likely to be 'Thunderbirds' or 'Ghostbusters'. Once I lived next to a family whose children spent much time in their garden. I think the parents had some religious pretensions; at any rate over the hedge I frequently overheard rich dialogue from the children involving angels and the devil in addition to a glittering range of more earthly characters. These 'games' were characterized by a total and extended involvement of the players. They happily negotiated their respective roles, and the events which were to take place, switching in and out of role to effect the planning. The same story sequence would be repeated again and again.

While the most absorbing dramas come into existence when the children themselves assume roles, similar processes may deploy puppets or other people symbols. My two oldest children played a game called 'towns', in which a whole metropolis would be created from bricks, boxes, and so forth. A cast of residents had their own cars and jobs. The game consisted of running through events in the life of the community such as burglaries, traffic jams, crashes and pregnancies. A toy representation of each character was not always thought to be necessary; the children became actors in the town as they chose. Solitary play can echo something of this; my youngest at the age of three explored for herself ideas about an afterlife by creating a 'Duplo' Hades, with a raised dais on which a reclining toy female person was said to be 'Mrs Jesus'. Subsequent events were difficult to interpret, and their underlying theology would probably not have met with Vatican approval.

In the infant classroom, teachers, well aware of the power of these processes, transform the 'house corner' into space rockets, castles, jungles, forests, estate agents, recording studios, shops of all kinds and hairdressers. 'Dressing up' clothes may figure as additional stimuli, rather more frequently in nursery and reception classes than elsewhere. Sand and water trays, construction toys and dolls houses are thought to provide related opportunities.

Despite this imaginative attention, in the majority of classes these activities are regarded as extra, as something that 'good' children can choose when they have completed their proper work. A corollary of this attitude is, of course, that the teacher herself would very rarely plan to be present in the house corner or its more exotic equivalent.

Is this because of problems in classroom organization? 'What will the others be doing while I am having this splendid time with children in the house corner?' the harassed teacher will inquire. Certainly, the teacher often seems to be attempting the impossible task of being in five different places at once.

Yet most 'normal' teachers in the 1990s plan, albeit for brief periods, to engage with *some* of the children in their class rather than with all of them at once. But it is very unlikely that they will be 'playing' with the children in any sense. Much more probable is that they will be hearing readers, helping with writing and spelling, and assisting with aspects of basic paper and pencil number work (Alexander, 1992).

We are confronted, then, with unmistakable current evidence that teachers even at Key Stage 1 do not regard the engagement of children in socio-dramatic play as having much of a priority compared with the three Rs, or 'covering' the National Curriculum, at least in the core subjects. Later in this chapter, we discuss ways in which story and play might be harnessed to help children build key elements in their understanding of mathematics. The suggestions are quite impossible to implement unless the teacher is prepared to spend some time with small groups. Several ideas are very appropriately handled with the whole class, but others are not. They will entail the teacher spending continuous periods of at least five minutes with a small group in the jungle, pirate ship, travel agents, or whatever, while other children are working independently. There will always be challenges in this situation so long as primary schools are basically staffed on the 'one adult in charge of thirty pupils' principle.

Now some readers might be inclined to use ideas just as they are presented here. With luck they might enjoy some short term success. Unfortunately, with this narrow construal of the material they would at best be in possession of a limited number of modest points of departure, whereas they really need an indefinite supply of fresh themes. At worst the chosen idea might well not work as it stands with a particular set of children, and our whole approach might be rejected for that reason.

In fact we hope for a very different reader response. Ideally people will take from this book a set of principles, and will feel empowered to develop their own activities with their own pupils in the light of their particular school situation. We certainly aim among other things to indicate a good range of starting points, but these will need to be thought through, transformed and developed by individual teachers to suit their own classes. The next two sections in turn discuss story and socio-dramatic play in general terms. We focus on specific classroom applications for each of these in the remaining sections of the chapter.

## Story

In chapter 2 we referred to the rich 'cognitive map' which is required in order that children can make the connections necessary to find their way around mathematics. Part of that cognitive map can be explained if we consider what a large part of thinking is sorted out in the mind by each person linking new experiences to old by 'storying'. That is, we take the new idea on board and fit it into another situation or set of situations which we remember. For example, driving for the first time in a fog, you might tell yourself 'My dad said that the first time he drove in a fog he jolly nearly had a bad accident because he was going much faster than he thought. The fog seems to distort your sense of speed.' Glancing at the speedometer confirms that this story was correct and you slow down. As well as beginning to introduce the notion of learning by storying, this example also indicates that the actual experience — in this case driving in a fog — is often needed before the 'story' is absorbed into knowing, in this case more about driving sensibly.

Thinking by internal storying is not a new idea. It has a long history and is generally accepted as being one way in which we make sense of our experience. Sometimes the story occurs much more quickly in the mind than the time it takes us to describe it. I have lost my umbrella. In my mind a picture forms of where I saw it last — hanging behind the door in my office and as I am at home I shall get wet. At other times the strategy is deliberately employed. A teacher, having lost an important letter, began to panic. Calming herself after an extensive search of the classroom she began to tell herself the story of the morning's activities; a narrative in temporal order. What had left the classroom in that period? The answer was the register and the missing letter was found.

These are short stories. Often they are more elaborate and as Wells (1987) points out, they are the means by which, through conversations, 'each one of us is inducted into our culture and comes to take on its beliefs and values as our own.' Young children, Wells (*ibid.*) suggests, even before they begin to talk, build up a picture of their world based on their experiences of it. Storying, he suggests, in its beginnings 'is not a conscious and deliberate activity, but the way in which the mind itself acts.' Later, it becomes more conscious as children learn how to share the narrative form which is the basis of both childrens' and adults' conversations. By the time children come to school most of them, even if they speak little (to teachers) are adept at making sense of the stories which they hear.

These stories, it must be emphasized, are not just stories from books (although their value cannot be overestimated). Try listening to almost any conversation and you will find it peppered with narrative. Many meanings are shared between the participants of a conversation otherwise communication would be impossible. Where much experience is shared, stories become elliptical to the point of being incomprehensible to outsiders. For example, a family joke may only require one or two words (say 'Aunt Eliza') to conjure up the story shared about Aunt Eliza which can illustrate exactly what the person naming her has in mind. Where fewer experiences are shared — as in a classroom — stories have to be more explicit. What is being suggested is that teachers can capitalize on a fundamental way of making sense of experience which is storying by quite deliberately using stories, i.e. using narrative forms as a setting for teaching.

In suggesting that storying is a way of thinking and of sharing meaning, however, we are not implying that psuedo stories should be used when young children are taught mathematics. That is, there seems little value in, for example, talking about 'Mr Square or Miss Circle.' (This notion would run into mathematical problems in any event as two-dimensional shapes cannot actually do anything.) What is being suggested is that in conversation with children, teachers should try to help children to apply their experience to the mathematics they are learning through narrative. Similarly, teachers can set up situations so this can happen. An example given by Brissenden has a shopping context.

*Simon*:   'I bought cheaper things.'
*Takuto*:   'What is cheaper things?'

> *Simon:*  'It means less money, because if you have less money. . . . Suppose if somebody had one pound and if you had 50p and you wanted to buy the same number of things you just have to buy cheaper things.'
> (Brissenden 1988)

In either case, talking with children or setting up situations, we are referring back to chapter 2 and the need for children gradually to acquire ownership of a complex network of concepts and facts. The teacher's role may include asking children questions but her aim is that children shall ask them and try to provide their own answers. To this end, a teacher can set up contexts where she and the children become involved in stories which enable them to think and apply experience to a concept or problem. These contexts include the teacher deliberately planning stories about the mathematics she wishes to teach.

The settings and content of such stories need not necessarily be about anything other than a wholly imaginary situation. It can be argued that experiences in school should, in so far as possible, be real. That is, what is done in school should either deal with things happening out there in the 'real world' or address 'real' problems in school. In this argument estimating the number of chairs needed for the concert has a value which does not exist in an imaginary problem. Although we would not dispute the value of this sort of experience we would argue that stories which are not 'real' in this sense are equally valuable and perhaps more importantly are easily constructed. Moreover, it is false to suggest that school itself is not real. All of life, including the life of the mind, is each person's reality. It is also a pity to see school and out there in the 'real world' as separate or divorced from each other. (See chapter 9 for more discussion of the 'realistic mathematics' issue.)

The sorts of stories which teachers can employ in teaching mathematics will be described but first we must distinguish between an imaginary problem of the sort found in text books and those we mean. Textbooks do sometimes attempt to be user friendly by setting up story situations. Various animals may illuminate the text or the heading of a page states that there is a sale so that every price given for the items illustrated must have 3p deducted from it. The point to make about textbooks and work cards is that in the solitary situation of the printed page learning can occur but may be less likely to do so than in the interpersonal situations we suggest. We are not disputing the value of commercial schemes and the like for necessary practice and revision. However, if a scheme and only a scheme is used, it is very hard for a teacher to know whether any learning which takes place can actually be used and applied outside of the scheme. In mathematics it may be necessary to redress the balance between the solitary situation and social settings in favour of the latter. This is not easy but in our view worth a serious attempt.

## Drama

It is quite easy to treat dramatic presentations as copies of everyday life. One of the common sense characteristics of dramatic activity is its make-believe quality, the sense that drama is 'only pretend', that it is playful and unreal. The implication of such a view is that drama in some way mirrors the world, that it is a reflection of a world 'out there' which is real and abiding and 'given'. Drama is meaningful and educationally valuable in that it mirrors the world accurately and gives children the chance to play at being what they are not. Their contributions are successful when they are life-like and the measure of success is the degree to which they can faithfully reproduce everyday experiences. However, even when they are successful the outcome is not to be taken too seriously (in the way that everyday living is serious and 'real in its consequences') and their work is easily dismissed as 'only make-believe'. Clearly, a teacher who sees drama in this light is likely to encourage the children in their pretence by helping them to copy the language and actions of those about them; helping them, as it were to mimic the world. Anyone who has tried this approach with young children is soon aware of the difficulties they experience in trying to reproduce speech and actions in any kind of life-like fashion. Their actions can be awkward and mannered and their speech stilted and lifeless. They may act like people in borrowed clothes and they present very vividly the dangers of models of teaching and learning based on copying and the transmission of knowledge.

### Drama and Everyday Experience

Such a view, though, may mistake the nature of everyday life as well as the opportunities provided by dramatic activities. The everyday world is not just there to be experienced (or copied) but is managed from moment to moment and sustained by the work done by those involved to present to one another situations which can be 'shared in common' and recognized as, for example, shopping or arguing or teaching. People are put in place through the manner in which they contribute to a social context and in the way they are treated by others. Teachers and pupils are described by their language and in their actions and by the way in which they address and engage with one another. The content is 'indexed' in their talk and their talk is made meaningful within the context they have managed to present and sustain. This 'reflexive' quality in everyday engagements brings out the active, collaborative and negotiated aspect of human experience and contrasts with a common sense view of the social life in which the world exists around us (and will continue to exist after we die) and in which the teacher's task is to show the child the world (and the way the world is) and to check the child's knowledge against the facts of life. If everyday life shares the managed quality of 'lived through' drama and is not simply 'given', then it is possible to see drama not as an imitation of life but as another aspect of the never ending business of making life visible and meaningful. The everyday and dramatic contexts are managed, both are 'make-believe' and the interesting question is not how does drama relate to everyday life, but how is it that we manage to indicate to one another that we are presenting dramatic rather than everyday experience. That is a question for another occasion, though. Here is a small extract from a piece of drama in which young children are working in the 'living through' dramatic mode; a teacher in role is trying to find out what he will have to do in order to be accepted as a member of a community living at the foot of a great volcano. The children, as members of the community, are putting him in the picture.

| | |
|---|---|
| *Teacher*: | 'What would I have to do to be able to come and live here?' |
| *Shirley*: | 'Believe in our god and do our ways.' |
| *Julia*: | 'Believe in our god and do our ways.' |
| *Ian*: | 'Climb the great mountain and if he doesn't, he won't be one of our people.' |
| *Mark*: | 'Learn to live like we do.' |
| *Teacher*: | 'Is that what I have to do? Did all of you have to do that . . . at one time . . . or do . . . don't you have to do it?' |
| *Mark*: | 'Yes.' |
| *Shirley*: | 'We will when we get older.' |
| *Teacher*: | 'Mmm . . . you'll have to climb the great mountain?' |
| *All*: | 'Yes . . . Mmm.' |
| *Teacher*: | 'And as long as you get down all right, you're a member of the group?' |

| | |
|---|---|
| *All:* | 'Yes . . . Mmm.' |
| *Ian:* | 'We . . . we're true people 'cause . . .' |
| *Mark:* | 'Yes . . .' |
| *Ian:* | 'Our . . . fathers and mothers were and if we go up now we'll probably be safe.' |
| *Teacher:* | 'I see . . . but me being a stranger . . .' |
| *Ian:* | 'Mmm . . .' |
| *Teacher:* | 'Would I have to do this?' |
| *All:* | 'Mmm . . . yes.' |
| *Julia:* | 'You'll probably have . . .' |
| *Teacher:* | 'Well, I'll have to give some thought to that because . . .' |
| *Bev:* | 'If you don't, you've got to go . . . to go away to another country.' |
| *Teacher:* | 'Well, I realize that so I'll have to give . . .' |
| *All:* | 'Mmm . . . Yes . . .' |
| *Teacher:* | 'It a bit of thought.' |
| *Julia:* | 'Mmm . . . Yes.' |
| *Teacher:* | 'Before I decide whether to go or not.' |
| *Some:* | 'Yes.' |
| *Shirley:* | 'And then you'll have to build your own house.' |
| *Teacher:* | 'All right.' |

(Millward, 1988).

This is not a representation but a creation of life; it is new-minted and those involved know no more about the way in which it might develop than they would in a similar engagement in everyday life. It shares few of the qualities of 'putting on plays' (there is no audience, no director, no rehearsing, no learning of lines, no plotting of moves), but it does have many of the qualities of everyday life. It is spontaneous, generative, original and purposeful, and the children and their teacher draw on the skills they have developed through the management of countless engagements in their lives. They are mindful of one another and attentive to the developing context and they contribute in ways that are appropriate and that will serve to elaborate and sustain the context. Their interactions even contain the interruptions, the inconsequentialities and the infelicities of everyday desultory talk and it is quite clear that they are not putting on plays but living through their drama. They are actively attentive to one another and to the developing context of which they are a part, they are engaged in their own learning and they are responsible for generating and sustaining the contexts of their learning.

Andrew Davis, Peter Millward and Deirdre Pettitt

## The Dramatic Presentation of Experience

The teacher who can encourage young children to engage in 'living through' (Bolton) type drama in the classroom (as well as in the playground) may be rewarded with a very different kind of teaching context. Involved in the drama and work in role, he or she is likely to develop relationships with the children which give them richer opportunities to take an active and interpretive part in their own learning. An easily recognized feature of the rather sad (and familiar) exchange from Andrew Davis' school days is the narrowly defined IRF formulation (Sinclair and Coulthard, 1975) in which all the rights are securely with the teacher, who initiates the exchange and who evaluates the child's response. All that the child can do is respond and that response, even when correct, is usually quite minimal. The emphasis is upon displaying knowledge on the teacher's terms, and the child is constrained to act in a surreptitious manner (and risk being chastised) in order to take some responsibility for the development of learning and understanding. Producing exchanges like this as teachers and pupils, is part of the management of teaching contexts and they cannot be simply put aside by good intentions. It is easy to see, for instance, how teaching of this kind reflects the transmission model (in which the teacher has extra rights as a result of his or her superior knowledge) but perhaps not quite so easy to appreciate how difficult it can be to break out of engagements with this quality and yet still be treated as a teacher. Teachers and children can do in drama what they cannot do when engaged in presenting the everyday reality of the classroom. In their drama children can, as a matter of course, initiate exchanges, change topics, interrupt and contradict. They can be experts upon whom the teacher is dependent (and really dependent if he or she is concerned that the drama should flourish) and they can walk away from the drama whenever they want. As in everyday life, the contributors to dramatic contexts must talk and act appropriately as they are attentive to the context they are concerned to construct and sustain. This puts very real constraints on the teacher, who is likely to be even more concerned that the drama should flourish than the children. When the teacher decides to work in role as, say, the foolish milkman/milkmaid, or helpless stranger, and when his or her concern is to sustain the identity of the foolish milk seller, then extra rights are given to the children who, through their expertise, hold a candle to the teacher/milkperson's folly and help us all to see the role for what it is.

Another lesson quickly learned by the teacher who encourages young children to present life dramatically is that the dramatic context is presented out of the children's experience of living. The teacher cannot make children present experience dramatically (though they can be made to take part in a play) and they cannot be told what to say and do (in the way that they might be directed to behave for a school assembly). If the drama is to flourish, the teacher has to contribute to a context which is part of the group experience and within which each of the participants feels at home and knows what counts as an appropriate contribution. Dramatic engagements are sensitive to the children's knowledge and experience; they are attentive to their world. The children are a part of the context of their own learning and are no longer looking in from without or trailing along in the steps of their teacher. It is from within contexts of this kind, dramatic or everyday, that the children have the opportunity to use their knowledge to realize their purposes. Furthermore, they know the world differently in doing this.

### Drama and Mathematical Knowledge

'Living through' drama is, like the presentation of everyday life, part of the business of making the social world visible; part of the business of making it meaningful. It gives those involved the opportunity to treat one another in accordance with the developing context and it means that they draw upon what they know rather than what they do not know. These features should help us to consider the value of drama in the development of mathematical understanding.

One is entitled to ask, of course, how drama can be used to develop mathematical understanding in young children but it might be better to wonder how children's mathematical knowledge can be used to create dramatic contexts. The first concern of the teacher must be to look after the drama, for there can be no development of mathematical knowledge through drama if the children are not contributing to, and living through, a rich dramatic context. After all, there is little point in using the drama to simply replicate examples taken from a mathematics scheme ('Will you be the person who. . . . Now who begins? What does she say?'). Rather, the contributions which draw upon the participants' mathematical knowledge must serve and elaborate the drama. The milkseller will look foolish as he or she is shown to have an inadequate grasp of number, and the more successfully the children can use their understanding of mathematics to confound the outcome of the milkseller's folly, then the more foolish will he or she seem. The milkseller's foolishness is presented through the children's wisdom, and the teacher has to work within the context in order to bring out the children's expertise just as surely as they have to indicate the milkseller's folly in their contributions. Of course, the children are getting an opportunity to make use of their knowledge of number, but it is the way their knowledge of number illuminates the context that is important. It is making their knowledge of number a feature of their managed social experience. This knowledge is not just something they use in their lives but it is also a part of their lives.

Before considering directly the way in which the children's knowledge of mathematics can be used to illuminate their drama, it is worth noting that by encouraging children to present experience dramatically, the teacher may be helping them to appreciate the part they play in the construction of contexts which they find meaningful and within which they feel at home. It encourages them to take an active role in presenting, and making sense of, their lives, and it seems likely that children who are used to working like this may find it rather easier to engage in the kind of mathematical thinking which Andrew Davis writes about. In the same way, Gavin Bolton's view of drama as a 'problem solving' activity (Dorothy Heathcote describes drama as a 'man in a mess') seems to lead very easily into an approach to mathematics which treats it as part of the way through which we manage to make sense of our lives. It encourages children to make their lives meaningful and not just look for meaning in the world about them.

A little later in this chapter we will consider a selection of ideas for dramatic engagements which can be developed to provide children with the opportunity to draw upon their mathematical understanding. However, before we get too precise, it might be helpful to consider three general approaches to drama which teachers might like to consider when trying to encourage young children to use their mathematical knowledge in the dramatic presentation of experience.

*Dramatic contexts based on mathematical knowledge*
It is possible to create dramatic situations in which the participants' mathematical knowledge is used to present the overall meaning of the context. The silly milkseller is an example of this. The milkperson may be pretty stupid in many ways, but it is his or her mathematical foolishness which is presented here and which drives the dramatic action. It is not all that has to be done, of course, for the participants have to present the milkseller, show what it means to want milk, cope with and present messages, demonstrate their own expertise and so forth. Indeed, all aspects of the situation are presented in the participants' talk and in their actions and they appreciate what is going on as they manage

to construct, and respond to, the dramatic context. After all, there is nothing luring beyond what they say and do, beyond what is recoverable from their contributions. We can keep on saying what is happening but unless it happens here, before our eyes, and unless it keeps happening and unless we talk about it and get a sense of a 'shared' in common context, then all of our huffing and puffing will count for nothing. The teacher is in the participants' hands, and everything is up to those involved and the silly milkperson will come alive in the light of their mathematical contributions. It would be quite possible for them, of course, to go on to present another dramatic engagement in which the milkman's foolishness comes of his inability to read properly or his poor memory. It would also be possible to create a drama about a doorstep milk thief in order to account for the strange responses to the children's requests for milk.

It is important to appreciate, as well, that at the heart of the dramatic engagement a tension has to be developed between those involved or between those involved and the context of their involvement. In this case the tension is provided by the teacher asking the children, through their roles in the drama, to overcome the milkseller's silliness and thereby get him to provide the right number of bottles. The tension is presented in the relationship between the children and the teacher in role as the silly milkperson. Without this edge of tension the engagement would look very like a bland copy of everyday life; it would not be dramatic.

## Mathematical knowledge applied to dramatic contexts

Sometimes young children might draw upon their mathematical knowledge in order to fulfil other demands in the drama. For instance, a group of early years children were busy trying to placate a very angry Tom Thumb who, through their teacher, was sending them tiny notes of complaint about the way in which they had (inadvertently) burned his house in their bonfire. They had agreed to build him a new house and this meant drawing up plans which met with his approval (very difficult to get) and at every stage taking account of his size ('about as big as your teacher's thumb'). All kinds of discussion and argument about the suitability of available materials in meeting his requirements were warranted and the children had to keep taking account of his size in developing their ideas and getting his approval. Clearly, the more they wrestled with the problems (and the more the teacher made it manageably difficult for them to do so) the more Tom Thumb and his predicament was made apparent. The children's mathematical knowledge may have been only one element of their response to Tom Thumb's predicament, but it clearly worked to mark his stature and to indicate their expertise and to put them in place as people who needed to make amends.

Sometimes the children might have to make use of their mathematical knowledge to prepare for the drama and Paley (1981) gives a nice example of a group of infant children spending a lot of time building a proper physical context for their drama. The drama involved a giant and a wizard, and it was very important to the children that each house was represented by an appropriate number of mats (more for the giant than for the wizard.) Getting the houses right for the drama meant a lot for the children and they were not prepared to proceed until this was done to the satisfaction of all. Of course, the decisions they made at this stage, based on their understanding of size, would affect the drama throughout its course. In both of these examples the children are getting the chance to make use of their mathematical knowledge and to make it work in their world as they draw upon what they know to meet their purposes. However, their mathematical knowledge and the use they make of it is part of their presentation of a dramatic context which is visible, meaningful and shared in common. They can enjoy what they have done with their knowledge, and they do so as Tom Thumb, the wizards and the giants are brought to life.

### Drama as a background to mathematical activities

It is also possible to use drama as a setting or background for mathematical work with young children. Drama can provide a purpose for mathematical activities and an incentive to complete them. The children could be engaged in a quest to find a missing prince, for example, or a box of dreams. All kinds of hazards could be put in their way, and the children may be asked to negotiate physical dangers (roaring cataracts, endless sands) and deal with awkward people who dream up a host of different challenges and tasks which they have to complete in order to proceed with their quest. Some of these challenges and tasks could be of a mathematical nature. Such an approach has the advantage of allowing the teacher to choose the kind of mathematical work he or she wants the children to do without the need to fold it directly into some kind of dramatic context. It has disadvantages, though. Clearly if the teacher tries to get too much out of these mathematical tasks the link with the dramatic context (which, in any case, is likely to be quite tenuous) will be broken and the children will be left high and dry doing mathematical activities. There is also the danger that the drama will be treated as a bit of fun around the mathematics and both areas of experience are likely to suffer for that. Finally, and most important of all, because the mathematical activities do not directly elaborate the dramatic context (and there is only the requirement that the children should complete the tasks properly in order to proceed with the quest) the dramatic activity cannot serve to help the children make sense of their mathematical knowledge. They may as well be back in the classroom, doing their sums. This may be the easiest way to use drama, but it may also be the least rewarding for the children and for the teacher interested in drama and mathematics.

If teachers are to use the children's knowledge of mathematics effectively in their drama and to make good use of drama in order to develop children's mathematical skills and understanding, they have to be aware of the way drama works and the opportunities it offers. They need to know what counts as an appropriate contribution to a dramatic context and how to set up situations so that children can make use of their mathematical knowledge.

So far in this chapter we have reflected on the power of drama and 'storying' in general terms. How might young children's mathematical invention or construction develop when properly informed by these ideas? Our answers begin with stories, for teachers already will feel confident that they can 'catch' children with these; start where you are, and extend by a series of judicious steps. We then proceed to examine instances of mathematically-tinged drama and dramatic play.

## A Start to the Use of Stories in Mathematics Teaching

Most teachers, very sensibly, have a repertoire of action games and singing rhymes which introduce early mathematical skills such as counting, addition and subtraction. A few examples will suffice (bearing in mind that local variations are legion).

Counting:

> One, two, three, four, five,
> Once I caught a fish alive,
> Six, seven, eight, nine, ten.
> Then I let him go again.
>
> Why did you let him go?
> Because he bit my finger so.
> Which finger did he bite?
> This little finger on the right.

*Andrew Davis, Peter Millward and Deirdre Pettitt*

Subtraction:

> Five little ducks went out one day,
> Over the hills and far away.
> Mother duck went quack, quack, quack,
> But only one little duck came back.

> How many left, etc.

Addition:

> One elephant was balancing,
> Round and round on a piece of string.
> He was having such enormous fun,
> He asked another elephant to come.

> How many now, etc.

These rhymes are invaluable and children love to do the actions and take on the roles. But, perhaps they are not as valuable as they might be if children know, as they sometimes do, the words but not the concepts. Here the teacher can use an existing and familiar story, i.e. she does not have to make it up, and elaborate on it to explain the mathematics that is being learned or practised.

For example:

*Teacher*: Let's sing the song about the little ducks. Do you remember what happens?
*Children*: They got lost. The mummy couldn't find them . . . (etc.).
*Teacher*: Yes, but she knew how many she had to start with.
*Children*: Five.
*Teacher*: How did she know there were five?
*Children*: She counted them.
*Teacher*: But ducks aren't very good at counting. How could we help her to remember?

Children may suggest making number labels for the ducks, thus introducing number recognition into the game. The ducks can be called One, Two, etc. (Ducks are not very imaginative when it comes to names for all those children.)

After the ducks have been selected and have chosen their numbers:

> *Teacher*: Mummy duck, can you put the little ducks in the right order?

After this has been done:

> *Teacher*: I know, lets play some tricks on the mummy duck. Shut your eyes mummy duck. Now she's not looking, one of you hide. Now mix yourselves up. Mummy duck, open your eyes. Can you tell which duck is missing?

(If the child sensibly says Fred, remind her that the ducks are called One, Two, etc.)

You get the idea? The duck rhyme offers opportunities for many extensions: changing the number of ducks, having two good ones who come back together, thus altering the subtraction sum, having a naughty one who loses his label and so on. The idea of a naughty, silly or not-very-clever character is a ploy frequently used in research which can be translated profitably to the classroom. 'It is not me who is not-very-clever' helps children to chance their arms and puts them in the superior role in which they are the expert for a change. Children do not have to be bored by the duck game because there are so many action songs and rhymes which can be extended in this way. Nor do you have to do this all the time but as and when you think it would be appropriate. Having got the idea children will often suggest their own extensions and perhaps use the games in their play.

From this starting point you may venture into making up your own stories. A teacher quoted in *Maths Talk* (The Mathematical Association, 1987) whom many of us recognize as Zoe Evans from Devon, tells how she makes up mathematical stories using soft toys. With a group, she shows the children how the toys leave their homes, go out visiting, quarrel and make up, all the time introducing new groupings of numbers, simple addition and subtraction as a story. Zoe Evans' work is not limited to early number or to number alone but permeates her first school. Some of her stories and games are available commercially (see references).

The rest of us may not be so skilled as storytellers but collecting some props will be helpful. For example, the old-fashioned flannel graph or similar props made from felt or card lend themselves to stories, especially those about the language of length. Imagine a story told with these aids which features a terribly tall thin princess, a fat cat, a long thin dragon, a prince who is shorter than the princess, three magic hoops: one tiny one, one larger than that and one very big indeed.

> 'Once upon a time, in a far away country, the king and queen were very sad because their only child, Princess Augusta was very very tall.'
> (Show the King, queen and princess. Say 'How do you know she is very tall?')
> 'They were sad because they liked her as she was but she needed a husband to help her rule the country after them and some princes are not keen on tall wives. The princess got fed up with these silly young men. She went into the palace garden to talk to Herbert, her cat and Ponsonby, her pet dragon.'
> (Show these cut outs and discuss the fatness of Herbert and the length and thinness of Ponsonby.)
> 'Herbert was a magic cat. He gave the princess three gold hoops. He told the princess if she stepped into the tiny hoop she would shrink, into the big one and she would get taller and the middle one would make her the same as she was now.'
> (By having two more models of the princess and some sleight of hand these changes could be demonstrated and discussed.)
> 'The princess got on Ponsonby's back and flew off, high into the sky to seek a prince who she might like to marry.'

This is episode one. At each point the teacher brings the children into the story, incorporates their ideas but emphasizes the language of size and its comparative nature. This story could run and run. However, it would be nice if the princess' final choice didn't even notice how tall she was. Once an effort is made to compose and tell the initial story the children themselves can play with the characters and make up their own plots, hopefully employing the mathematical language introduced.

Puppets can be used in stories in the same way. One teacher borrowed her daughter's knitted Snow White and the Seven dwarfs, sewed numbers on the dwarfs and used them for number stories to great effect. For example, naughty ones hid and had to be identified or they got mixed up and had to get in line to make sure each took their medicine. History does not record what her daughter thought about this but teachers' children are well used to the appropriation of their property! The more serious point is that telling stories about mathematics to young children needs things that they can see and touch including, of course, themselves as actors in the drama.

## Drama and Dramatic Play: Mathematical Examples

We now consider examples of the use of dramatic play for learning mathematics. Pupils should make a personal contribution to the development of the activities, having scope to choose their own level of contribution, and some freedom as individuals to continue to build up their mathematics on the basis of their current knowledge. Contrast this with the requirement of a 'transmitter' who would want the pupils to slot into a prescribed sequence at a prescribed level.

Such group work cannot be expected to be wholly successful if occurring largely without the presence of adults. Children cannot generate mathematical structures unaided. They require initiation into mathematics already present within adult society.

Clearly the teacher will wish to foster specific areas of mathematics; a key role will nevertheless be the creation with the children of a story context . . . a set of characters with motives and problems. As was seen above, often a tension will be induced, which the children will be motivated to resolve. Where the teacher is not interacting directly and continuously with the children, she will still wish and need to intervene in the independent play which may stem from scenarios she has initiated. Many children do not 'play' in these ways without considerable prompting. Moreover, some are constrained in their imaginative explorations by media images. These may be valuable in providing children with initial scenarios and characters (or in many cases, caricatures) but without intervention the media influence may fossilize dramatic play into a restricted number of rigid patterns.

### *Working with a Group to Create a Story Context*

The first scenario, described in some detail incorporates quite un-ashamedly hackneyed elements; so long as the children have sufficient ownership of subsequent developments no apologies need to be made for this. In terms of the earlier classification, it belongs to the second category — a dramatic context based on mathematical knowledge.

Begin with a few pieces of equipment such as a cauldron, spoon and wand. Ask children for some more suggestions. Establish the character of a 'bad-tempered magician'. Then you need to make a crucial move; explain the bad temper in terms of a mathematical deficiency. The magician (for instance) cannot say, read or write numerals (presumably the victim of some tiresome spell . . . ). This presents the children immediately with a problem to solve, or a context for invention.

But how does the teacher engage the attention of a lively group of infants to do this? One obvious answer is to go immediately into role; to pick up the wand and use a special voice, and to explain her problem directly to the children. Children who do not readily speak in a group can often make excellent use of puppets, which may be used to project their personalities without incurring the same social risks. There is no reason why a teacher who initially feels less than confident about going into role should not try a puppet as spokesperson; what is certain is that the children will be very appreciative.

The magician has assistants; children might suggest 'cats'. The magician proceeds to explain that she has to earn her living despite her deficiencies. Children again may contribute ideas about how magicians earn their living; the teacher will need to have included the thought that there are spells to be carried out, and ingredients for these spells, which have to be counted carefully or they will not work properly. All this might still be possible with the teacher in role.

In discussion, and initial play with a group of children, ideas about how the numerals are to be communicated can be explored. Perhaps the magician points to items, and makes appropriate numbers of sounds on a tambourine, xylophone, claps, waves her wand, etc. If possible, the teacher will manoeuvre developments in such a way that the importance of the assistants acknowledging receipt of the messages is recognized. Perhaps the 'cats' must turn round the same number of times before putting the right number of frogs, etc. into the cauldron.

So the mathematical objectives attainable include the development of simple counting and matching. Of course, given different kinds of constraints on the magician, other mathematics might be encouraged, and possibly at a more advanced level. The teacher wishing to lead this drama can think carefully in advance about such constraints, and the mathematics which seems most likely to stem from them. With slightly older children, for example, perhaps the magician can't say numbers less than ten . . . and must find other ways of expressing them. The children themselves, if the activity is handled as recommended, will have a fair amount of freedom to create alternative explanations of the magician's bad temper. Some of these will not be mathematical at all. It will be hard to predict the mathematical terrain which might be traversed in later developments. This does not matter, so long as the teacher keeps a careful account of what has taken place, especially if she is, for whatever reason, anxious about time and 'getting through' relevant National Curriculum programmes of study.

As indicated above in the context of developing rhymes and stories, going into role and make believing some weakness or stupidity, with the children cast as experts, is a ploy which many teachers of young children include in their repertoire. Clearly it should not be over used, but it can be a powerful tool for the stimulation of mathematical thinking.

Note other potential in this scenario. Echoing the 'silly milkman' activity, we might have the magician's cat who can't count . . . and always puts one more spell in the cauldron than is asked for. This part of the story can be acted out, with the magician's response. Children can suggest other ways in which the cat might be silly, and these too can be 'played'.

With some children, the teacher might suggest that the magician is clever enough actually to proceed on the assumption that the cat will make a mistake. The children discuss and then act out what the magician should say to anticipate the rule-governed mistakes and complete the spells successfully. Hence, when magician wants five worms in the cauldron, she asks for six, etc.

We might abandon the 'bad tempered' character, and decide instead that the magician is grossly overworked. Nevertheless, she is very kind to her assistants, so they all wish to help her as much as possible. For example, certain simple spells only require eight items, which must be either slugs or spiders. (Children discuss, and possibly make spell ingredients, such as snails, worms, spiders, and the like.) They then make up 'spell books' containing all the possible recipes. So, to infest your neighbour's garden with garden gnomes requires six snails and two slugs, or five snails and three slugs, and so on. Perhaps there is a scene when the books are presented to the magician . . . on her birthday? She might try out the spells. Do they all work?

In another twist of events, the magician's magic for increasing and decreasing quantities is not efficacious, but her kind cats want to help her maintain the fiction that it is. For a 'doubling' spell the magician puts four worms in the cauldron, and says her spell. While she is asleep, the cats ensure that there are eight by the time she comes back to check. Groups of pupils could suggest other 'changing' spells that the magician might require of this type, and again could act them out. Perhaps they do NOT always get it right, but the magician's arithmetic is excellent, various complications might ensue, some of which have further mathematical potential.

A scenario for Y2 and Y3s could involve the lost book of Animal Spells. All the magician can remember is that it is some aspect of the *number* of ingredients which is significant; spells made with numbers with a given property transform victims into such and such an animal. Perhaps numbers in the two-times table will achieve transformation into a frog. A group of children might be set to make decisions about these matters. They could revise their knowledge of which numbers are in which 'tables' by colouring in multiples on a 100 square. Twos, threes and fives could be tackled, at least. Armed with this knowledge, and the patterned 100 squares available for consultation, the children decide on a number property which is to be the key factor for a given spell. (The degree of teacher intervention here will have to depend on the capabilities of the children.) They then allow the magician (by this stage a child is playing this role, we hope) to try out spells on them, miming transformations appropriately, so that the magician can try to rediscover her lost spell recipes. Children could discuss what other number properties could be used for this kind of game.

To mention other avenues very briefly . . . there might be currency devised which can be spent in a special supermarket; ingredients and spell books could be on sale; the 'money' could be used. There would be the usual learning opportunities here, but also additional areas because the children have been involved in inventing the whole thing . . . including, for example, the relationship between one coin and another. Perhaps one is worth three of another. The shopkeeper may turn out to be a cheat. The children might decide to create a magician bank. The magician takes cheques to the bank and obtains currency. Perhaps a cash dispenser could be simulated. Special cheque books and credit cards could be made with further dramatic possibilities.

As was said earlier, there are dangers in spelling out possibilities in this way. It also may seem to imply a degree of teacher control which we are not ultimately advocating. Indeed, because this book is about mathematics, the mathematical elements have been highlighted. Yet the mathematics must not dominate or control the dramatic/play possibilities or it may crush them. We must bear in mind the general discussion of drama earlier in the chapter. The mathematical construction or invention will only be at its best if the activities achieve their own momentum in the children's terms. Even within a very closely defined structure, the children can still be given appropriate freedoms to interpret characters and develop the consequences of events in such a way that involvement is maintained.

The teacher, then, might well be in role to introduce some of these ideas. She need not dominate, however. Clearly the magician has the most 'important' part in the above scenario. Later, for the sake of generating momentum in the drama, it might be appropriate for pupils in turn to take this job on, and 'order' the teacher to carry out activities as assistant or whatever. A teacher observing an activity of this kind largely in the hands of a group of pupils, may then be able to assume the mantle of a subsidiary character to encourage exploration and construction of a specific set of mathematical concepts.

## Further Ideas for Stories and Dramatic Play

Here are some other starting points for stories and dramatic play. They are not elaborated in totally comprehensive detail. The hope is that they will serve to spark the intended users into producing their own ideas suitably tailored for the children with whom they are familiar.

*Gnomes*
Gnome ideas are not original to us. Unable to credit the source, we can only apologize and acknowledge our gratitude to the anonymous donor(s). The gnome collection represents a different genre from the socio-dramatic play of the magician. We have a 'subcreation' (Tolkien, 1964) . . . a fictional world, initiated by the teacher, peopled by characters of a certain kind. Pupils, probably older than those involved in the magician scenarios, invent further details of this world through discussion and investigation. Dramatic play is less likely, but there is plenty of 'story making' and in a whole range of senses, construction. Considerable language work, both spoken and written, could well arise in connection with such a project. The teacher provides the initial definition of the situation, in which key features or constraints provide the potential for mathematical problem solving.

Somehow set the scene for a community of 'gnomes.' What do they look like? Could the children pretend to be them? There might be a chief gnome. The gnomes arrive in a new country and decide to set up a village. Gnome houses are to be made from four multilink cubes. Gnomes insist that no one house is like another. The houses are on plots which are large quadrilaterals, each of which is different from all the others. This stage would be carefully monitored and stimulated by the teacher, especially where the terms 'different' and 'same' were discussed. The houses are displayed together in the 'gnome village'. How many gnomes can live in the village, given their sensitivities about domestic architecture?

The quadrilateral plot idea could be replaced by another. Perhaps each house will have a lawn exactly twelve square units in area. Each lawn must be a different shape. Children's designs could be recorded on squared paper. The gnome houses could be placed on a very large grid. Details of houses, using grid references, might be sent to the chief gnome planner. The cost of painting houses could be raised. One face of a cube costs ten pounds. Which is the most expensive house? Which the cheapest? The local gnome authority may require plans of the houses . . . different elevations, and so forth.

Do gnomes play football? If so, they require a pitch whose dimensions are appropriately proportionate to their stature. Top juniors with calculators and appropriate teacher assistance should make some headway here.

Each gnome has a car. They like swapping cars, and do so at the beginning of each week. But they don't like doing the same swap again more than is absolutely necessary. Only one pair of gnomes can effect a swap in any one week. The gnome Mayor convenes a committee to explore how many weeks will elapse before they have to start repeating swaps. What happens with different gnome populations? In further developments with older juniors, the pupils may well be able to pose mathematical problems for themselves arising from the gnome world.

Some more 'contexts' are now listed, and described more briefly. We begin with situations particularly suitable for the younger age range. Referring again to the earlier classification, these mainly instance the idea of mathematical knowledge applied to dramatic contexts.

*Teddy Bear's picnic*
Preparing food, drinks for given numbers, setting places, etc. Perhaps introduce the unwanted visitor. Relevant mathematical ideas/terms will include 'too many', 'not enough', and so forth. Or the character who is never there on time. There might be a greedy bear who wants one more cake than the others. The children will be counting, matching, exploring and practising number relationships. The teacher's role would be to join in the play from time to time, establishing characters, counting routines, etc. which the children will, in all probability, make their own and try out when the teacher has moved on.

*Master chef with assistants*
He/she issues commands to fetch so many items, e.g. cooking utensils, food, to stir so many times, to leave something on the ring while they count up to so many. Perhaps provide containers half full of such and such, or half spoonfuls. The house corner can become the restaurant kitchen. The teacher's role would be judicious intervention in role, as before. Tension can be injected with mathematical repercussions, if a

sudden influx of guests is postulated, a vital ingredient turns out to be past its 'best before' date, or a cake is to be made for a competition.

### Bus/train/boat/space ship journey

So many chairs in rows act as bus seats. The maximum number of standing passengers might be stipulated. Bus driver issues tickets. Money might be used. There could be a sequence of stopping points. Naughty passengers could insist on boarding when there are already the statutory number standing. Perhaps fares relate to the number of pick-up points. A passenger refuses to pay, or has forgotten her purse. Teacher role as before.

### Masters and robots

This exemplifies a dramatic context based on mathematical knowledge. Children take roles as 'masters' (or any other non gender-specific word suggesting someone who controls a robot!), and as robots. The 'master' demonstrates an action, and then indicates how many times the robot is to perform it. She might indicate by saying a number, showing a number, showing a card with spots, making that number of sounds or by some other means. The robot picks up another card indicating that he has understood the signal. So, for example, he is shown the numeral 4, and picks up a card marked with four spots, proceeding to take four paces. As usual, we need an element to induce dramatic momentum. Might the robot become rebellious? Perhaps the robot has various kinds of malfunctions. These could be mathematically systematic, in a fashion analogous to the silly milkperson of chapter 2.

If the commands were extended to include directions about left and right turns, then the activity could encourage thinking about angle, direction and shape in addition to counting *per se*. Clockwise and anticlockwise might be tackled. Probably the teacher would introduce this activity with the whole class, possibly in the hall. Opportunities might then be provided for the children to play at this activity independently.

### Cafe

Props . . . tables, chairs, plates, cutlery, menus, play dough food. Children act as staff and as customers. Waiters share out, e.g. sausages, for diners. Idea of fair shares, or so many each, or 'grown ups' getting more than 'children'. Menus could include the labelling of dishes with large numerals, Chinese restaurant style, for recognition practice.

Bills could be created and paid for by customers. This again is the standard 'house corner' play, with teacher intervention in role to encourage the mathematical elements among others. Dramatic possibilities with mathematical implications include incorrect bills given to customers, inappropriate responses to orders, greedy customers trying to gain more than they have paid for, etc.

### Ghost

The teacher tells the story of a shy and lonely ghost who comes to join an established spook community in the 'castle' set up in the house corner. She has been frightened of the number three ever since her sister ghost was bitten by the ghost of a fierce dog with a large number three hanging from its collar. So messages have to be exchanged with the ghost, involving numbers, without mentioning three. 'The number after two . . .', 'before four . . .', etc. Castle 'doors' might be set up round the classroom. Established ghosts have their 'homes' by these doors. The story line must develop the necessity for communications with the new ghost. For instance, the ghost who lives by door three invites the newcomer to tea, etc. Perhaps an invitation is sent, bearing the dreaded number. Children could be invited to speculate on the likely reaction of the new ghost, and perhaps act this out. So they discover she is frightened of three, and send a revamped invitation, which says: (Children discuss what should be said.). Perhaps the party begins at three o'clock. Possible developments: other numbers for various absurd reasons which children might cook up could become taboo, and the communications more complex in consequence!

This situation might be created by the teacher with the whole class in discussion. It lends itself both to independent 'play' and to the provision of opportunities over a period of several days for children to talk together about possible plot development, with regular reporting back to the whole class.

### Toy cars and roads

Set up a typical floor activity with an assortment of toy cars, perhaps a cloth road layout, bricks, traffic signs, toy people, etc. The mathematics can include routes, right/left, clockwise/anti-clockwise on roundabouts, traffic queues for ordinal number . . . my lorry is the *fourth*.

Join in the game from time to time, making use of appropriate number and spatial language, and encourage the same in the children. The joining in should be genuine, rather than a series of questions such as 'What colour is the *fourth* lorry?' and the like. A dramatic element, as usual, is most likely to result in 'successful' games. Encourage the development of characters, with problems of some kind, and the playing through of a plot which involves, among other things, travelling from one place to another on the 'board'.

*More Demanding Activities: Y2 Upwards*

*Robbers and sleeping villagers*

Initial story: Villagers are all misers and keep trays of gold coins under their beds. Robbers creep in at night and try to steal treasure. They must not take too much, for the trays are magic and scream if the number of coins falls below a certain level. (Or if the number left is an odd number, a prime number, etc. As always, the appropriate number properties will depend on the attainment levels of the pupils concerned.)

Groups of two or three 'villagers' must plan secretly what the rule will be. This might have to be done in class as part of the preparation for the drama, and checked through with the teacher. Evidently the 'coins' will have to be made in advance; plastic money is not very exciting in this context. During the dramatic play in which the burglaries are enacted, villagers must apply the rule and provide the 'scream' from the tray when appropriate. This will presumably involve them in pretending to be asleep, but watching the robber burgling their tray and noting how much is being taken. The trays could be designed on a large-scale and take the form of ten by ten grids marked from 1 to 100. This would allow both robbers and villagers to keep careful track of what was going on.

The robbers will try to steal as much money as possible without getting caught. They must also note the rule being applied, so that they can do better next time. They may take several burglaries to discover the rule. Perhaps there could be a convention that robbers who are 'caught' four times must stop burgling. Robbers might need to work cooperatively, pooling knowledge gained from previous crimes, ultimately enlisting one burglar to go for the mother of all crimes, agreeing on some way of sharing the proceeds.

To begin this activity, the teacher tells part of the 'story', invites contributions from pupils to develop it further, and organizes and initiates group planning to facilitate playing through the 'drama' which eventually takes place with the whole class in the hall. Suitable props might be used, as usual.

*Estate agent*

Transform a corner of the classroom into a branch of an estate agent. This will involve large numbers for house prices. Accordingly, some initial discussion of large numbers and how they are written and spoken would be appropriate. The activity itself involves further practice along these lines. Children could make 'plans' of rooms in houses. They could construct a simple database of available houses; this could be entered on the computer. 'Searches' could be carried out for customers. Perhaps the houses could be made from card or construction kits. Entering and accessing information on a database figures in Attainment Target 5 of the National Curriculum.

### The 'auction'

Children are first introduced to the idea. Decide on what is being sold to fit in with the topic, perhaps furniture, houses, jewellery. Children could be given 'cheque books'. The teacher might have to play the auctioneer initially, to give pupils the idea. Pupils could then take over. Further complications could include pupils becoming 'buyers' with a fixed amount of money with which they must try to make maximum purchases.

# 4    Teachers Constructing Mathematics

*Brian Woodhouse*

## Introduction

Given that resources for the professional development of teachers are becoming increasingly scarce as LEA INSET provision wanes and funding is channelled through local management of schools (LMS), less expensive, more efficient and accountable methods are being sought to help and support teachers, often through school-centred or school-focused activity. The improvement of teachers' subject knowledge is widely acknowledged as of central importance, if primary schools are to make the progress demanded with teaching the National Curriculum (OFSTED, 1993). Additionally, there is a need for schools to provide more consistent quality teaching and learning models for student teachers to witness as more training is transferred to classrooms.

A constructivist view of the teaching and learning of mathematics would suggest that such INSET would embrace, as a fundamental tenet, teachers, both individually and with colleagues, constructing or reconstructing their subject knowledge, building on prior understanding in ways unique to them, thereby being better prepared to help children do the same.

An over-reliance on commercial scheme materials and/or textbooks would then be avoided as teachers and pupils become more mathematically empowered through an interactive exploratory approach to the subject. Those primary school teachers who lack confidence in their mathematical ability or perceive mathematics in terms of remembering and using prescribed rules and procedures, should benefit from a development model based on mutual sharing and the support of colleagues, which encourages teachers to work in an effective learning environment, promoting experimentation, questioning, reflection, discovery, creativity and discussion. Learning mathematics can then be presented as an involvement in process, an interpretation and performance of emergent facts, concepts and procedures rather than the traditional mastery of a body of delivered knowledge. Consequently teachers can then be released from mathematical content as a first focus of their concern.

## Discussion of an Example

To exemplify some of these considerations, an exercise offered to a number of in-service courses for primary teachers is described. A single sheet of A4 paper and a pair of scissors are given to each participant who is then merely invited to cut the paper. When no further clarification is given but everyone is encouraged to proceed, the results and indeed attitudes are interesting to observe. The ensuing cuts can be variously described as: tentative — a short anxious snip usually symmetrically placed along and at right angles to one of the sides; flamboyant — raking thrusts creating ribbons of paper; inventive — studied cuts creating intricate patterns; perverse — a dismissive cut chopping a minuscule triangle from one corner; the list could go on. A suitable vocabulary to describe the results is then sought and what emerges is a series of variables as the differences and samenesses of the results are considered. The number, type (curved, straight, multi-staged), length, location and angle of cuts are identified as *operative variables* while the original shape of the paper, folding or not before cutting and even whether to use scissors or not are examples of values of *context variables*.

What does this introductory and at first sight trivial activity achieve? The participants have been placed in a situation where there is a choice of action, a decision to be made and subsequent analysis to be conducted of the types of possible choices available. All contributions are equally valid and discussion and communication are promoted. Minds are now better prepared to explore new approaches and a first step has been taken in initiating mathematical activity not just imitating the mathematics of others.

Returning to the exercise, it is quickly realized that there is no (mathematical) interest in allowing all the variables to be in play at the same time. The application of constraints (presetting the value of some of the variables) defines a number of problems of differing appeal and levels of difficulty.

One such activity is to consider a single straight cut through the paper and identify the polygons so formed. The operative variables are the location and angle of cut. A classification of the polygon pairs is then undertaken (Figure 4.1) and certain special cases, using additional constraints, are examined (Figure 4.2).

*Figure 4.1*

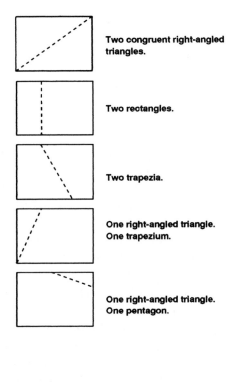

Two congruent right-angled triangles.

Two rectangles.

Two trapezia.

One right-angled triangle.
One trapezium.

One right-angled triangle.
One pentagon.

*Figure 4.2*

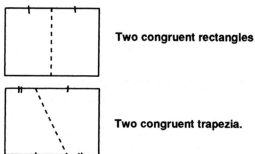

**Two congruent rectangles**

**Two congruent trapezia.**

It is appreciated from the analysis that there can be an infinite number of different cuts producing polygon pairs which lie within a single class. For example, in Figure 4.3, all cuts from A except AC produce a trapezium and a right-angled triangle. There is a dynamic dimension in play here. The trapezia and triangles formed from cuts intersecting the sides BC and CD have different orientations.

Figure 4.3

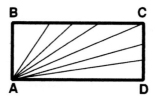

These non-static positions contrast with those normally seen in text-books or on the blackboard. Gattegno (1958) saw the value of 'freeing minds' from the 'conditions put by the restricted field presented.' The activity is in fact similar to his rectangular geoboard usage but offers a different embodiment, i.e. a variation in both the mathematics and the material. This accords with the Perceptual Variability Principle (Dienes, 1960) whereby the same conceptual structure is presented in the form of a number of 'perceptual equivalents' to allow scope for variations in concept formation for the individual learner.

A powerful idea emerging from the exercise is that of exhaustion. Given the constraints, can all the different polygon pairs be found within the defined classification? This question demands a systematic attack on the problem to ensure that all five classes emerge. One successful strategy is to start at an arbitrary point on the perimeter of the rectangle and see what happens when the angle of cut is varied. By moving this point along the perimeter and choosing 'representative' positions, in each case examining the effect of changing the angle of cut, an exhaustive strategy is guaranteed. In other problems involving exhaustion, e.g. when investigating all possible ways of filling a three-sectioned ice-cream cornet, given say four available flavours, an elementary knowledge of combinatorics can be useful and indeed offer an opportunity for a first exploration of simple permutations and combinations.

After investigating simple decompositions of a rectangle, the situation can now be reversed to initiate a second exercise in that by recombining the polygon pairs, equal side against equal side, figures other than the original rectangle can be produced. An example is shown in Figure 4.4.

*Figure 4.4*

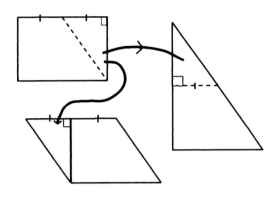

Again, discussion of possible constraints prompts questions such as whether it is permissible to flip over one of the shapes before recombination and if the parts must be coplanar (lying in the same plane). If 'flip-overs' are allowed, and coplanarity demanded, some interesting combinations emerge. A worthwhile pre-activity is to try to anticipate the recomposed shape. Three figures in addition to those shown in Figure 4.4 can be made (Figures 4.5, 4.6 and 4.7).

*Figure 4.5*                         *Figure 4.6*                         *Figure 4.7*

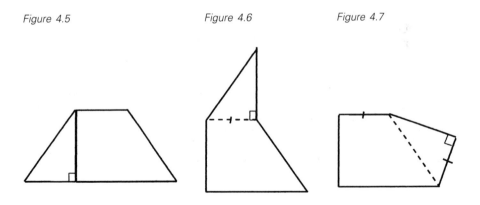

The recombinations deserve individual study:

Figure 4.4 reveals similar triangles and a special case of the mid-
point theorem. (The straight line joining the midpoints of two
sides of a triangle is parallel to and one half of the third side.)
Figure 4.4 also offers a parallelogram and brings to mind a general
method of finding the area of any such shape.

Figure 4.5 is an isosceles trapezium and,

Figure 4.6 is an example of a concave pentagon

Figure 4.7 is an unusual convex pentagon in that it contains three
right angles.

All the transformations are examples of area conservation, the area
of each shape being equal to that of the parent rectangle. The six
figures exhaust all possible cases under the given constraints. The idea
can now be extended to each of the five classes from the first exercise
and to special cases in which pairs of equal sides are deliberately
created (Figure 4.8).

*Figure 4.8*

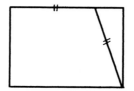

This example offers an interesting contrast to the cut proposed in figure
4.4. Again, six reconstructed polygons are possible (including the parent rectangle): a convex pentagon with three right-angles, a parallelogram and an isosceles trapezium as before, but a quadrilateral with two
right angles (a surprise?) and a second convex pentagon, this time with
two right-angles.

Having looked at two examples, each of which produced six different recombinations; it is interesting to pose the question which cuts
would produce the maximum and minimum numbers of different re-
combined figures. This last is shown in Figure 4.9.

*Figure 4.9*

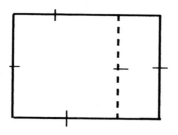

Note that in this case there is only one recomposition — the original rectangle.

Arising from an initial single cut of the paper, several quite different mathematical routes can be taken by considering other values of the variables and different sets of constraints. A selection, initiated by non-specialist teachers attending in-service courses, are listed below:

(a) Symmetries (reflective and rotational).

When work of this type was introduced to children at Key Stage 1, multiple sets of shapes were pre-cut and made up in stiff card. Early learners, including reception class children, were able to appreciate an impressive range of properties of plane figures through decomposition and recomposition activity.

(b) Angle properties, an interesting example of which is an exploration of right-angles in figures. A series of challenges for a Y6 class constructing various polygons with given numbers of right-angles arose from this activity.

Figure 4.10: *A convex pentagon with three right-angles*

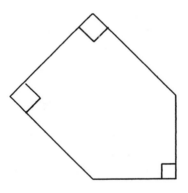

(Can the figure be constructed with none of the sides equal?)

Even the simple task of constructing a quadrilateral with four right-angles produces lively discussion regarding rectangles, squares, diamonds and areas and ratios of linear measures of similar figures.

(c) Different starting points, e.g. parent figures other than rectangles.

(d) Tessellations using shapes arising from a curved line cut across the rectangle.

(e)  A single fold to produce a silhouette (an overhead projector is useful for this exercise) and the classification of silhouettes arising from different folds.

Figure 4.11

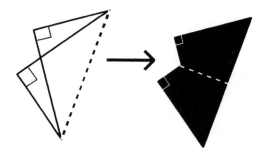

Here, the fold is along the diagonal of the rectangle. The resulting figure is a concave pentagon with two right-angles and reflective symmetry.

(f)  Folding the paper before making a single cut under selective constraints.

Figure 4.12

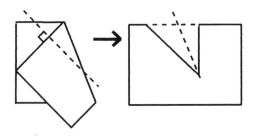

Two figures are formed: a scalene triangle on which the original fold is an angular bisector and a concave heptagon with five right-angles. This exercise provides many surprises, particularly if attempts are made to predict the results before cutting and unfolding.

(g)  Multiple folding before making the single cut. Special cases of this activity give familiar repeating patterns.

(h)  Single folds to produce given fractions of a rectangle.

Figure 4.13

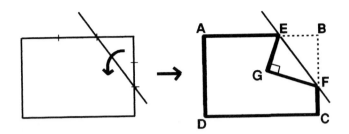

In this example, both the length and width of the rectangle are trisected and a single fold made as shown. The area of the heavily scored concave hexagon AEGFCD is 7/9 of the original rectangle. [ (1 − (2 × 1/9) ]. Additionally, the folded triangle EFG becomes 1/8 of the area of the convex pentagon AEFCD.

Similarly, using a 4 × 4 partition (16 units of area) and reflecting a corner of area $1^{1}/_{2}$ units of area, the area of the resultant concave hexagon is 13/16 of the original rectangle and the triangle is 3/29 of the convex pentagon.

An examination of the mathematics potentially emerging from these exercises indicates unexpected coverage of the plane geometry (excepting the circle) included in the programme of study for Key Stages 1 and 2. Given the starting point — a single cut in a sheet of A4 paper — teachers look back over their work and its progression and are usually surprised by the powers of creativity and understanding they have displayed and the opportunity they have taken to reconstruct their own knowledge of two-dimensional geometry. Their knowledge of the subject may be somewhat patchy but the impact of these practical exercises can allow the new experience to interact with the old and, as new insights are discerned, provide an impetus for further study.

The series of activities prove accessible to everyone at the start, allow challenge and extensibility, invite decision making and involve speculation, hypothesis making and testing, definition, reflection and interpretation. These characteristics echo the ingredients considered as necessary for a 'rich mathematical activity' cited in the curriculum development study *Better Mathematics* (Ahmed, 1987).

**Recasting Standard Objectives**

The above analysis spawns a number of mathematical opportunities within different subject areas of shape and space (symmetry, angles, tessellations, polygons, fractions) from a simple starting point. The same techniques can be used to develop rich classroom activities to meet specific mathematical objectives, for example as defined by statements of attainment in the National Curriculum. A possible initial procedure is to take an approach, currently used by a teacher to meet a named objective, often a teacher-led set of activities or a section of a commercially published scheme, and recast the work in a more exploratory mode.

Consider, for example, the objective 'knowing and using addition and subtraction facts up to 10'. A traditional activity to support this is to partition sets of objects in different ways and then record the results in the form of simple number sentences. A discussion of context will furnish various possibilities: real objects, pictures, structural apparatus, coins, measures, in fact typical settings offered by published schemes. What can be changed in the format number sentence itself?

Clearly, the numbers in the frames, the number of stages, the operation(s), the number of sentences and their possible interaction can all be regarded as operative variables. Constraints would include:

(i)  A restricted set of number from which to choose, e.g. even or odd numbers only, one even number and one odd number, one number repeated.

(ii)  A given result, e.g.

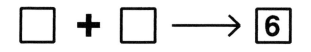

(iii)  A given starting point, e.g.

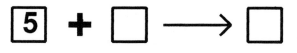

(iv)  Given numbers in a multi-stage sentence, e.g.

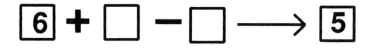

(v)  Mixed operations, e.g.

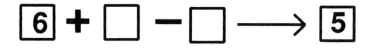

(vi)   Interacting or comparable sentences, e.g.

Figure 4.14

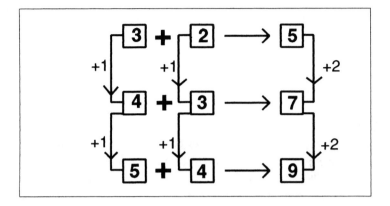

To exploit these dynamic situations, frame boards can be constructed with number and operation cards used in accordance with constraints decided by the teacher or the child. Examples of this which involve combinations of constraints are (a) and (b) shown in Figure 4.15.

*Figure 4.15:   Frame boards*

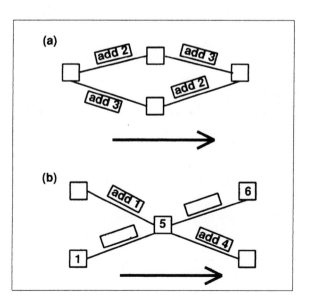

Attempts can be made in most of the above cases to find all possible sentences for the given set of constraints. Although the permissible set contains numbers less than 10, a remarkable range of difficulty levels emerges.

There is of course no need to define a context and the work can be developed under the heading of investigating within mathematics itself.

## Conclusion

In trialling some of these ideas in school, teachers have commented that they themselves must reappraise their own and children's mathematics through their interactions with children, just as children in their turn interactively construct their knowledge. This would appear to support a view of school mathematics based on the principles of constructivism (Steffe and Wiegel, 1992). This reappraisal is sometimes uncomfortable as it may require deconstruction of some of the 'mathematical baggage' that all teachers take into their classrooms. A reconsideration of what is thought to be known and understood can create uncertainty and unpredictability in situations previously felt to be controlled. Some strongly believed procedures and concept structures may need to be abandoned or modified and rebuilding attempted. There is some evidence to suggest that this happens to teachers from a wide range of mathematical experience, not just to those with the least mathematical preparation (Goldin, 1990).

In this brief chapter, a view is offered of INSET experience, the orientation of which is process rather than content together with the structuring and sequencing of the learning environment, and which is based on a constructivist appreciation of both the teacher and the pupil as learners.

A few strategies are presented, arguably simple but important, which encourage a focus on how learners can make sense of their mathematics and how these understandings shape the learner's mathematics behaviour (Schoenfeld, 1988). Although a considerable amount of investigative styled material is available to primary school teachers, little work appears to have been done in analyzing either the processes involved in mathematics learning associated with 'investigations' or the particulars of efficient related teaching strategies. It may now be profitable to search for further strategies which could assist teachers to construct their own mathematics as opposed to being merely consumers and imitators of the subject. In this regard, the processes of oral and written communications of such constructed mathematics to peers may be worth examination. It may also be worthwhile revisiting 'the modern heuristic' (a study of the process of solving problems especially the mental operations typically useful in this process) (Polya, 1945) and attempt to translate the reasoning where appropriate for primary school learners.

Whatever strategies and skills emerge, however, teachers must be given the opportunity to experience each particular strategy in different contexts and to practise associated skills.

# 5    Pattern in Constructing Mathematics

*Maria Goulding*

> Mathematics may be said to deal with the basic patterns that human beings find in, or impose upon, their environments . . . the way that [they] think about, communicate about, or learn to deal with these basic patterns (Davis, R.B., 1984).

The emphasis here upon human activity and communication fits in well with a general view of learning in which an active learner makes sense of daily experience in and out of school. Very young children bring to the school environment knowledge about the patterns that are taken for granted in their everyday lives. This is not just about decorations and naturally occurring forms, but about the underlying features of regularity and repetition which characterize events in the day, occur in stories or rhymes or songs, routines at home or school and so on. Using this knowledge children look for patterns and test predictions by observing and acting within a social situation.

In all their learning they will also need to adapt what they know in the light of new experiences, and some of the actions which they have used reliably in the past may be found wanting, even misleading, in seemingly similar situations. For instance, the child who has used sellotape to stick together paper models will be disappointed when using the same method to join up a model of wooden blocks. Sometimes it is patterns of social behaviour which are misread, as when an articulate child cannot understand the pained silence which follows her announcement that the man sitting opposite on the train is very fat. This process of adaptation is common in constructivist theory (von Glasersfeld, 1987).

In the more formal situation in school, the search for similarities, differences, repetition and regularity is common to many areas of learning but there are particular ways in which pattern is central to mathematics. In the following two mathematical examples, some of these ways are illustrated.

*Example 1*

In Figure 5.1 there are four numbers written in three different scripts. Can you identify them?

Figure 5.1:   *Other number scripts*

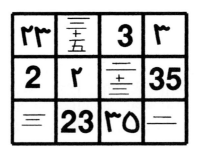

Different number scripts such as these may well be familiar to the pupils themselves and are beautiful examples of mathematics as a human product. The way certain symbols have developed clearly relates to the number represented, e.g. the Urdu symbols for 2 and 3, and the whole system has evolved as an efficient tool for communicating information about quantities, in response to the activity of trade.

In trying to solve the puzzle the reader may have:

(i)     grouped the scripts together on visual similarity,
(ii)    looked for patterns in the formation of the numbers,
(iii)   used the relationships between the values of the numbers by referring back to the known script.

Reasoning from these clues she may be able to identify the four numbers in the three different scripts. In doing so, she may also have been aware that the Chinese script differs fundamentally from the other two with its use of a separate symbol for 10, and with the vertical rather than horizontal arrangement of symbols. Despite these differences in culturally agreed systems of number, it is possible for someone who knows only one of the scripts to decipher the puzzle. The fact that representing counting numbers is an activity common to many groups partly accounts for this, but also significant is the recognition of reasonable patterns in the codes. Knowing one set of symbols helps us to recognize similar patterns in unfamiliar scripts.

*Maria Goulding*

### Example 2

The second problem may also illustrate how common ground can be achieved, in this case despite different ways of seeing a mathematical problem.

In Figure 5.2 the first three in a sequence of matchstick models are given. How many matchsticks would you need to build the 100th model?

*Figure 5.2:  Matchstick sequence*

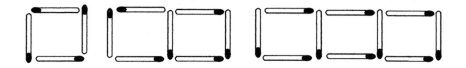

One person may notice that each time a new square is drawn three more matches are added. The sequence of matches 4, 7, 10, 13, 16 . . . may be continued until the 100th number is reached.

Another may say that in the 100th model there are 100 squares. Each square uses 4 matches giving 400 matches. Of the 101 vertical matches, 99 are repeated twice in the count. So the number of matches is $400 - 99 = 301$.

Yet another person may say that the first square counts for 4 matches and that all the others count for three, so in 100 squares there will be one counting for 4 and 99 counting for three.

So that gives $4 + 3 \times 99 = 301$.

These are only some of the possibilities. If any of the explanations are difficult to follow this may give the reader some idea of the difficulties which children experience in understanding the teacher's methods for solving problems.

The first of the three methods is laborious but if done correctly will give the right number of matches. It is probably less time consuming than drawing the 100 squares and counting the matches. The second two methods rely on finding a general way of looking at any shape in the sequence and finding a relationship between the structure and the number of matches, which could be applied to any of the models. Such methods are of wider application than the first but involve more sophisticated thinking, and some people may prefer to stick to the sequential method if they are more comfortable with it. This is a very common phenomenon which teachers will recognize as problematic, e.g. when children continue to add up using their fingers, when they fall back upon repeated addition instead of multiplication.

This is not to deny the value of pupils' personal methods of working which are often inventive and surprisingly sophisticated. In the research on pupils' 'own' methods for doing written calculations (e.g. Thompson, 1993) it has often emerged that not only were these methods successful for the pupils but that they revealed a great deal more about their thinking and understanding than standard methods. Sometimes, however, the teacher may want to present alternatives, or better still, share methods which pupils have come up with themselves amongst the group. I shall return to this later.

In both of these examples patterns and relationships have been involved in two principal ways:

(a)   when the objects studied exhibit patterns — the patterns formed by the matchsticks, the repetitions involved in the number symbols.

(b)   When the search for patterns and links is a strategy used to solve a particular problem.

If we think of the patterns involved in multiplication squares, tiling, statistical surveys, games of chance over a long run, and tessellations, to give but a few examples, then it is clear that pattern in the first sense is found in many branches of mathematics. Used in the second sense, as a mathematical process, we could find many instances particularly in investigative work. In the next section, where childrens' work is considered, it is this aspect of pattern which is the focus.

## Children Using Pattern in Doing Problems

When children encounter mathematical problems, there are several ways in which they may proceed. If the teacher has initiated the problem she may do a similar problem with them first and then expect the pupils to imitate the strategies that have been worked out already. This is a common way to proceed, and providing there is a degree of challenge in moving from the original problem to the new one then the pupils may be offered some degree of autonomy. If the new problems are simply variations on the original, with a few minor changes, and the teachers' method is clearly the expected approach then there is very little room for pupils to build upon their present understandings, develop new ones or make choices about strategies. Many of us try to strike this delicate balance between supporting pupils and offering challenges which means we are constantly using our judgment in interacting with pupils.

Although mathematical problems are many and various, a common feature is that present knowledge and skills are used within the often unfamiliar problem situation. This context may be 'real life' or purely mathematical: the teacher or the pupil may have posed the problem; during the solution pupils may need to learn new skills; new problems may present themselves during the solution. In many problems pupils will be trying to recognize parallels with previous experiences or trying to recognize patterns which will give clues as to which avenues to pursue. In the three situations which follow, children are working in this way.

(1) In this extract, (Goulding, 1993 also discusses this material) a ten-year-old pupil wanted to find out how to play music on the Roamer, a turtle like toy, programmable from a touch sensitive panel. This was a genuine problem for the pupil, who was branching out from using LOGO-like instructions to make the toy move. The teacher could have given this information:

The ♪ instruction has to be followed by two numbers.
The first number tells the Roamer how long to make the note.
The first number can be 1, 2, 3, 4, 5, 6, 7 or 8.
1 is the shortest, 8 is the longest note.
The second number tells the Roamer how high or low to make the note.
The second number can be 1, 2, 3, 4, 5, 6, 7, 8, 9, 10, 11, 12 or 13
1 is the lowest, 13 is the highest.

She could have demonstrated these rules along the way since the amount of information is too much to take in all at once. However, she decided to adopt a different approach and this is a reconstruction of the interchange taken from notes.

*Teacher*: 'What have you found out?'
*Alison*: 'You need two numbers. You can't use 9 first (demonstrates), but you can use it second. The first number has to be less than the second.'

(She keys in ♪ **7 6 GO**)

No, that works.
*Teacher*: 'Can you make a tune?'

*Alison*: (She keys in

♪ **24** ♪ **56** ♪ **78** ♪ **59** ♪ **34** ♪ **23** ♪ **45** ♪ **67 GO** )

'It's awful' (tries to sing the tune).
*Teacher*: 'What do you notice about the notes?'
*Alison* (Plays it again twice)
'High or low. How long.
For a high note, try a high number.'

(She tries ♪ **89 GO** )

'See, it's high.'

(She tries ♪ **78 GO** )

For a low note . . .

(She tries ♪ **12 GO** )

'. . . See'

(She tries **89** ♪ **12 GO** )

'The first is longer, it's also higher.
If you put in big numbers it's higher and longer.
If you put in smaller numbers its shorter and deeper.'
*Teacher*: 'You've tried two large numbers together. What happens when
you try a large and a small?'

*Alison*: (She tries ♪ **19 GO** )

'It's high and short. The 1 makes it short, the 9 makes it high.'

(She tries ♪ **27 GO** )

'That's a little longer, and a bit lower.'

(She tries ♪ **49 GO** )

'That's longer and higher.'
*Teacher*: 'What about keeping one number the same?'
*Alison*: 'What like?'
*Teacher*: 'Keep the first number 1.'
*Alison*: (She tries

♪ **19** ♪ **18** ♪ **17** ♪ **16** ♪ **15** ♪ **14** ♪ **13** ♪ **12 GO**

and listens to the sequence three times).
'It went down deeper and they're all short.'
*Teacher*: 'Can you get a run of notes all going up?'
*Alison*: (She tries

♪12 ♪ 13♪ 14♪ 15♪ 16♪ 17♪ 18♪ 19  **GO**

and listens to the sequence several times).
Then she tries a tune:

♪12 ♪ 13♪ 14♪ 15♪ 16♪ 17♪ 18♪ 19

♪19 ♪ 18♪ 17♪ 16♪ 15♪ 14♪ 13♪ 12

♪12 ♪ 13♪ 14♪ 15♪ 16♪ 17♪ 18♪ 19

♪19 ♪ 18♪ 17♪ 16♪ 15♪ 14♪ 13♪ 12

Although she has not experimented with the lengths of the notes she does seem to have cracked the idea that the two numbers have separate functions and this is confirmed when she creates a new tune:

♪19 ♪ 18♪ 17♪ 16

♪16 ♪ 19♪ 18♪ 17

♪17 ♪ 19♪ 18♪ 16

♪18 ♪ 17♪ 16♪ 19

♪81  **GO**

It needs to be stressed that this is not meant to be a model intervention. It is noticeable, for instance, that Alison continues to use 1 for the note length after the teacher's suggestion. The reader may have said different things at that point, or she may have told Alison to go off and explore some more. More likely she would have been interrupted by other pupils in the class. There are, however, some useful features which may be worth considering. First of all the pupil was coming to a new use for the Roamer and her previous knowledge could have been misleading.

When programming the Roamer to move: ↑ takes one input which can have more than one digit, e.g. ↑2, ↑26, ↑100 and the same is true of the curved arrow left or right instructions. Alison has obviously noticed something different at the beginning of the dialogue, as she has already found the restriction on the first input and the fact that two inputs are needed. She does not appear to have found out that the two inputs have different functions but rather than pointing this out straightaway the teacher has helped Alison to tease this out herself.

Alison's responses are also noteworthy. Her initial input is, with two exceptions, a series of pairs of consecutive numbers which may indicate a systematic approach to the investigation. She then proceeds to investigate the relationship between the numbers and the sound produced, and when she starts to input sequences she clearly uses patterns and permutations. Her approach is logical and systematic. In future work she can experiment with notes of different length and she may want to investigate patterns in the numbers which produce tuneful melodies. Work like this problem solving gives pupils opportunities to use and apply mathematics, and in this case has arisen in a musical context.

(2) In the second example, the problem has been set by the teacher, and is an example of a purely mathematical situation. Minimal introduction was made — pupils were simply asked to investigate routes travelling along the grid lines of a square grid from the bottom left corner to the top right. Rose's written conclusions after a short time working on the problem are shown in Figure 5.3.

The investigation, although unfinished, has been tackled in a systematic way by measuring the routes and then summarising the information, albeit incorrectly. The routes themselves are not drawn randomly, several pairs being mirror images of each other along a diagonal. Having drawn two repeats in the first part Rose decides to stop. She then uses her information to make a prediction about routes on a 3 by 3 square, and is able to see that this does not work — 'this theory is wrong'.

Investigations of this kind invite pupils to generate a set of patterns and to answer questions arising out of the situation. Pupils can be encouraged to work systematically and to present their findings orally first and then in the written form. Such activities are easy to find, but as in this case, they are not always sustained and developed. This may be for a variety of good reasons, one of which may be the problem of sustaining interest if the avenue being pursued is not very productive. This is a dilemma for the teacher trying to enable pupils to construct their mathematics which will be addressed more fully later.

Figure 5.3:  Routes

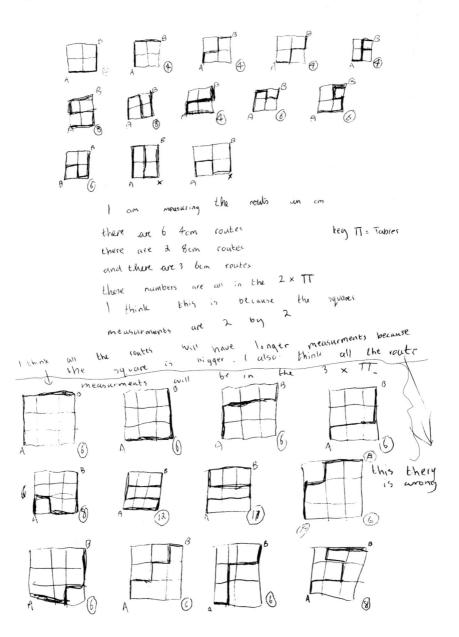

I am measuring the routs in cm

there are 6 4cm routes          key ∏ = Tables
there are 2 8cm routes
and there are 3 6cm routes
there numbers are all in the 2 x ∏
I think this is because the squares
measurments are 2 by 2

I think all the routes will have longer measurments because
the square is bigger. I also think all the route
measurments will be in the 3 x ∏.

this theory
is wrong

(3) In this last example, the teacher again sets the problem (see Billington and Evans, 1987) but finds herself moving the pupils on to extend it. Again we have an example of a pupil (only eight years old) using pattern at various points in the problem, and well able to communicate her solution in written form.

*Figure 5.4: Handshakes*

First of all Miss gave us a problem. it was that
of there were four people in the class and every
one has to shake hands with every other person
how many hand shakes will there be the answer was
6 this is how we got the answer The first person
has three people to shake hands with because he or
she must shake hands with their self the second
person has two people to shake with and the
Third person only has one person to shake with.

Then Miss gave us another problem it was if five
people where in the class how many hand shakes
would there be the answer to that was Ten that
one was easy we already had 6 from the other
problem now all we had to do was add on another
four because the fifth person only has to shake
with the other four so that's how we got the
other answer

Then Miss gave peter and I another problem
this time it was with 11 people when I got home.
I did it on paper first of all I got the answer
10 9  7 6 5 3  2 1  I added them up and
got the answer 43 then then the second time
I got  10 9 8 7 6 5 4 3 2 1  I added them up
and got  55. I added them up like this
first I got the ten and crossed it of to show that I
had used it then I got the 4 and the 6 I new that made 1.
10 so that made 20 then I got the 9 and  and that
made Ten so now I had 30 after that I got 7 and 3

and again that made ten after that I got 8 and two
then. last of all the 5 so' thats how I got 55.

Figure 5.5:  *More reporting on handshakes*

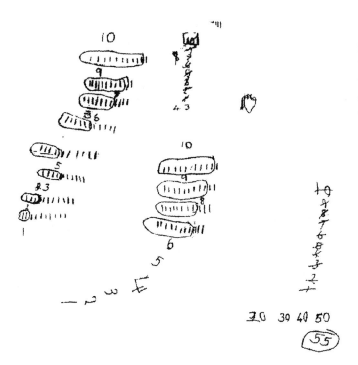

These examples were chosen to illustrate children thinking mathematically in a variety of situations. There was evidence of the children:

(1)  Recognising patterns.
(2)  Describing patterns and explaining the reason for them.
(3)  Asking questions.
(4)  Searching for patterns by exploring systematically.
(5)  Exploring links and relationships and seeing when these work.
(6)  Using patterns and relationships in arriving at solutions.

Not all features, however, were present in each piece of work. The use of pattern was clearly important, but because the evidence is limited we do not know what learning experiences have encouraged these children to work in this way. In the next section, we will move on to look at ways in which the teacher can encourage these aspects of mathematical thinking in her pupils by choosing or modifying activities, using the potential of her pupils as a social group, and experimenting with her own interventions.

## Constructing Mathematics in Classroom Situations

Rather than separate out the six features of pattern identified in the last section, it will be better to look for teaching implications in identifiable classroom situations. Inevitably the strands will interrelate, depending on the activity and the pupils' responses, so it would be artificial to treat them individually. Certain features, however, will be especially relevant at particular points in the following cases.

### *Teaching a 'Conventional' Topic*

*Making ten*
Instead of asking young pupils to do a variety of unconnected 'sums' using cuisenaire rods they could be asked to find as many ways as possible of making ten with two rods. This may result in an unsystematic set of combinations which can be discussed with the group (Figure 5.6). Each pupil could share her set describing them in any way she wishes:

'I've put two yellows together, then a black and a green. . . .'
'My first is a white and a blue, that's 1 and 9. . . .'

*Figure 5.6*

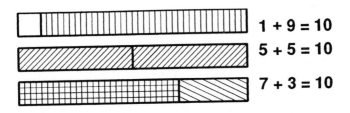

$1 + 9 = 10$
$5 + 5 = 10$
$7 + 3 = 10$

Some pupils will have made the same arrangement, or used the same pair of rods in a different order. If the pupils do not point this out then the teacher may prompt with:

'Has anyone made the same pattern?'
'What do you notice about George's set and LeeAnne's set?'
'Has anyone got a different set from everyone else?'

The teacher can extend the activity by asking pupils to pool their different arrangements and build a systematic pattern 1+9, 2+8, 3+7,

*Figure 5.7*

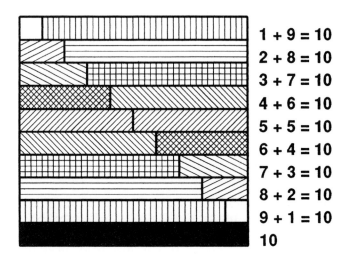

etc. (Figure 5.7). Just by looking at the shape patterns which emerge, it should be clear if there are any combinations missing and this omission would be a valuable opportunity for discussion.

Pupils can then be encouraged to describe the wall. They may notice how the first rod is getting bigger while the second is getting smaller, how the same pairs of rods appear but in different orders, how the joins look like steps, etc. If appropriate they could record the symbol sum for each arrangement, and be encouraged to notice patterns in the symbols. These observations could then be linked with the shape patterns in the wall so that the reasons for the patterns are made explicit.

This activity is designed to bring out the patterns in the number addition bonds for ten, and can be supplemented with calculator work, practical work with objects and money work using ten one-pence coins.

An extended piece of work with money could involve the use of all the possible coins (1p, 2p, 5p) to make 10p. Here the complete listing might be too time consuming for each individual, so groups could be asked to come up with five possibilities and then all of these could be pooled in a larger group. The question 'How do we know we have all the possibilities?' would be a stimulus to organizing the results systematically. Having each possible set of coins on separate paper plates would enable groups to classify them using different criteria and may reveal missing combinations.

*More number work on the wall*
Other relationships can be drawn out using the wall activity at a later stage. By looking at the whole wall the pupils may see that:

1+9 + 2+8 + 3+7 + 4+6 + 5+5 + 6+4 + 7+3 + 8+2 + 9+1 + 10 = 100

They can be asked to rearrange the rods in different patterns and to write the equivalent number sentence, e.g.

1+1 + 2+2 + 3+3 + 4+4 + 5+5 + 6+6 + 7+7 + 8+8 + 9+9 + 10 = 100

or

1 + 2 + 3 + 4 + 5 + 6 + 7 + 8 + 9 + 10 + 9 + 8 + 7 + 6 + 5 + 4 + 3 + 2 + 1 = 100

or

2×1 + 2×2 + 2×3 + 2×4 + 2×5 + 2×6 + 2×7 + 2×8 + 2×9 = 100−10

(One challenge might be to use one of their arrangements to find 1+2 +3+4+5+6+7+8+9= ?).

The reader needs to be cautious about homing in on the above examples because pupils will invariably come up with much more complex arrangements which demonstrate many other relationships (Figure 5.8).

Figure 5.8: *Not just a wall of rods*

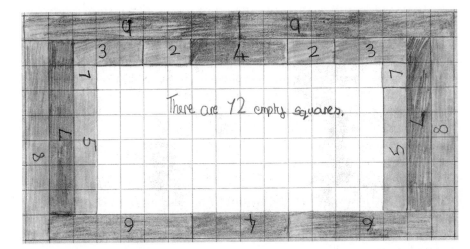

These are just as valid and as rich in possibilities if pupils are asked to describe the arrangements and the number relationships within them, e.g.

6 + 4 + 6 = 1 + 3 + 2 + 4 + 2 + 3 + 1
18 × 9 = 90 + 72

*Maria Goulding*

### Doing 'An Investigation'

Although investigative approaches may be used in many different situations, there are many sources of starting points, often called investigations. The routes along the grid from the previous section is such an example and will serve to illustrate aspects of the teacher's role in using such an activity.

In Rose's account (see 'Children using pattern in doing problems, Example 2') her starting point was to find the length of all the routes on the three by three grid. This is a very accessible entry point, since very little pre-knowledge is required, and as such could be used with a whole class. Here the fact that there are a large number of children is a positive advantage since between them they may find all the possible routes, and any errors in finding the route lengths can easily be checked amongst the class. Recording of all the possibilities can be done communally in a variety of ways:

(a)   Each table shares individual results and comes up with a set drawn on a large piece of paper. A whole class set is drawn by comparing the results from each group and eliminating repeats.

(b)   One pupil records and the other pupils give instructions without showing the recorder the route on the grid. These instructions could be descriptions of the route, e.g. it looks like a staircase, or step by step instructions, e.g. forward 1 turn right forward 1 turn left forward 2 turn right forward 1.

Knowing that all the possibilities have been obtained is quite difficult in this problem, unlike in the handshake example, so the pupils may be invited to sort the results in different ways to see if there are any missing. Time spent on comparing the routes by using mirrors and cutting the grids out and turning them is well spent since the ideas of reflection and rotation may be useful in finding all the possibilities for larger grids (Figure 5.9).

*Figure 5.9:   Reflection and rotation in routes*

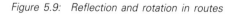
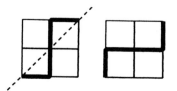

Once pupils are satisfied, they may start to look for patterns in the lengths of the routes. Again, time spent here in discussion is well spent. Rose, working on her own, noticed that the grid lengths were all in the two-times table and went on to test a conjecture. A big group will notice more patterns — for each length route the number of possibilities is even and goes up in two's, there are more short routes than long, or that the number of turns in any route is either 1, 2, 3, or 4. . . . The articulation of these observations is valuable in its own right but it can also be the stimulus for further exploration.

At this point there are different avenues which can be pursued, e.g. finding a link between the size of the grid and the number of routes, finding the longest/shortest route for different sized grids, finding how many of each length route in different sized grids, investigating rectangular grids . . . These questions constitute problems to be solved, and if the number patterns generated can be generalized then there are clear links with algebra. This abundance is both exciting and daunting, requiring the teacher to decide how she can help the pupils to move on.

One possibility is to stop the whole class before moving on to the other grids and ask them to say what they are going to do next and what they are going to investigate. This is important for a variety of reasons. Firstly, planning investigations is a skill which is frequently done for the pupils in excessively structured activities. Secondly, if pupils are going to construct new mathematical knowledge then they are more likely to sustain interest if they have chosen their own line of enquiry.

The teacher still needs to help keep the momentum going and to provide appropriate interventions. She may be aware that in the next square grid (3 by 3) there are very many more possibilities and that pupils may become bored quickly. At this point they could display a summary of their results so far, and invite contributions from other members of the class — 'These are the routes we have found. Can you find some more?'

They can return to the problem later. Meanwhile, they could either choose another line of enquiry or the teacher could suggest one.

If they had reached an impasse with the 3 by 3 grid, a different sort of experience would be gained by investigating the shortest routes on a variety of square and rectangular grids, trying to explain the result and then predicting the lengths of the shortest routes for new grids. There is a fairly straightforward relationship between the dimensions of the grid and the length of the shortest routes which can be obtained by spotting patterns in the numbers, but the real value of this activity would be in explaining why this relationship works in terms of the original problem (Figure 5.10).

Figure 5.10

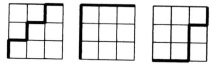

**Shortest routes on a 3 by 3 grid**

**Shortest routes on a 3 by 4 grid**

The teacher can then ask them to justify this so that they are all convinced that the relationship will always work whatever the dimensions of the grid.

It is easy to underestimate the amount of time required for pupils to fully explore a typical investigation and it is tempting to push them towards a result too quickly. A useful strategy is to make time for review sessions when either the whole class or groups stop work and go over what they have been doing. This gives them an opportunity to clarify ideas, to collect together results and to plan ahead. Sharing of work in progress also gives pupils the opportunity to communicate what they have been doing and to think about presenting their results to others. When the teacher feels that enough time has been spent a final whole class evaluation can be made where the progress of work from the starting point to the different end points can be shared. In this way, the class as a social group is constructing and evaluating their collective findings. The class is working as a mathematical community.

### Moving Pupils On

Pupils themselves may reach points when present understandings cannot be applied successfully to a new situation or when present methods are found to be effective but time consuming. If such a moment arises unexpectedly when a pupil recognizes a problem and wants to resolve it, so much the better. Alternatively, situations may be deliberately engineered by the teacher to expose errors or reveal limitations in the pupils' existing frameworks.

*Creating Conflict*

A common expression used by pupils and adults alike is 'to multiply by ten you add a nought.'

Some teachers would immediately put pupils right on this one and say something like:

> 'Well actually all the digits are moving to the left as they are becoming ten times bigger and we have to put a nought in the units column as a place holder.'

The trouble with that response, in my experience, is that pupils do not recognize why their own simple rule should not be used. This includes pupils who have a perfectly clear grasp of multiplication and could demonstrate the sum in question with apparatus. An alternative approach is to leave pupils uncorrected but to engineer situations later in which they can see that their pattern only works with whole numbers, and breaks down as a rule for multiplying decimal numbers by ten.

The teacher may start with lots of whole number questions and invite responses from the group:

$5 \times 10, 9 \times 10, 12 \times 10$

*Teacher*: 'You can do these easily. How about some harder ones? Use your calculators if you can't do them straight away in your heads.'

$98 \times 10, \quad 4{,}576 \times 10, \quad 3{,}456{,}789 \times 10. \dots$

*Teacher*: 'Is there a pattern here? How are you doing these?' (Pupils' answers accepted without evaluation.)

'What about $1.5 \times 10$?'

This may generate the answer 1.50 amongst others, in which case the teacher can use the conflict in the group as a learning moment.
*Teacher*: 'Shall we just check that on the calculator?'

At this point the teacher may throw the problem back to the pupils to explain. She may need to help: 'What does 1.5 mean?' 'Can you do $1.5 \times 10$ another way?' 'Can you draw a picture?' 'When does adding a nought work?' 'Why?' 'Should we look for patterns with other decimal numbers?'. . . .

*Maria Goulding*

## *Looking for More Efficient Methods*

*Use of the calculator*
Very simple starting points can often be very effective. Recently, some pupils in a mixed Y3/4 class I had been working with in school came to do some maths with me at the university and I had bought some felt tip pens (8 at 27p each) for them to use.

We sat round in a big group and I asked them to work out how much the pens had cost, with the aid of calculators. The several different answers were written up with pupils saying how they had arrived at the answer. Most of the pupils had used repeated addition with variable success, and a few had used multiplication. These methods were recorded as well. Then everyone checked through slowly together. The emphasis was not on arriving at the right answer quickly but on sharing the group's methods and looking for advantages and disadvantages. For instance, it was the pupils who pointed out that they easily lost track in the repeated addition method and that the multiplication method was quicker.

The activity led on spontaneously to looking at the relationship between the two methods when one pupil announced that you could do $27 \times 8$ or $8 \times 27$. This led to repeatedly adding 8 on the calculator. At first the pupils did not count their steps — they simply aimed for the target of 216. Later they all repeated the addition and verified the number of steps. One pupil now suggested repeatedly adding 4 to reach the target. A real situation had led to a rich mathematical activity which explored the relationship between repeated addition and multiplication and generated a whole set of equivalent patterns:

$27 + 27 + 27 + 27 + 27 + 27 + 27 + 27$

$8 + 8 + 8 + 8 + 8 + 8 + 8 + 8 + 8 + 8 + 8 + 8 + 8 + 8 + 8 + 8 + 8 + 8 + 8 + 8 + 8 + 8 + 8 + 8 + 8 + 8 + 8$

$8 \times 27$

$27 \times 8$

$4 + 4 + 4 + 4 + 4 + 4 \ldots$

The reader will be able to think of further patterns.

*Finding a new command in Logo*
Technology can be a powerful tool for pupils constructing mathematics as can be seen from the calculator use in the last example. Using Logo

on a computer has a similarly liberating potential with appropriate teacher intervention. One strategy is to teach pupils new commands and then demonstrate how they work, but another is to encourage work in which the need for a new command will come from the pupils. In my experience, the open task of drawing a picture often results in somebody needing to draw a circle. Pupils often think there must be a special command for a circle and are surprised that they can achieve a very close approximation by repeatedly moving a bit and turning a bit. This realization is often facilitated by asking pupils to walk out the circle away from the screen. When they return and start to type in

FD 1 RT 1 FD 1 RT 1 FD 1 RT 1 FD 1 RT 1 FD 1 RT 1 . . .

they usually ask for a quick way of repeatedly executing these two basic instructions from the pattern, and the teacher has a perfect opportunity for introducing the REPEAT command.

A similar opportunity for pupils with experience of Logo is to offer particular patterns as challenges (Figure 5.11).

*Figure 5.11: Concentric squares in LOGO*

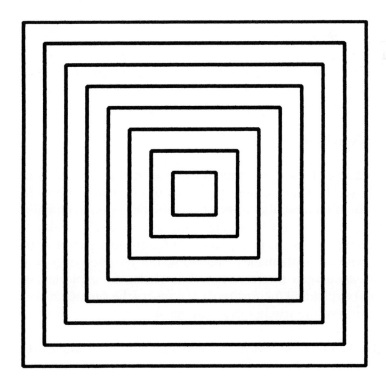

Here the pupils may start with a small square:

```
TO SQUARE
REPEAT 4 [FD 100 RT 90]
END
```

then they may get themselves into position for the next with something like

```
PU RT 90 FD 20 RT 90 BK 20
```

and move back into the editor to change the 100 in the square procedure to 140.

Pupils will soon realize the need for a procedure which will draw a square of any size and the time for introducing the variable command is ripe:

```
TO SQUARE :SIZE
REPEAT 4 [FD :SIZE RT 90]
END
```

```
TO STEP :MOVE
PU RT 90 FD :STEP RT 90 BK :STEP
END
```

The pupils may then try SQUARE 100 STEP 20 SQUARE 140 STEP 20 SQUARE 160. . . .

and further work may lead on to the introduction of the process of recursion.


## Conclusions

In this chapter I have interpreted the use of pattern quite widely but have chosen familiar mathematical activities to illustrate how it can be used to both increase the range of possibilities open to children and to encourage the communication and sharing needed to make it part of the learning process. It is important to realize that patterns abound in many common mathematical situations, but the class as a community can be encouraged to create new knowledge by exploring systematically and explaining their patterns in terms of the situations from which they arise. For the teacher this may mean:

(1) Setting tasks which will generate a lot of examples/data from the pupils.

(2) Giving time for regular discussion of this material, in which everyone's contribution is valued. Very often what is going on in the teacher's head is not the same as what is going on in the pupil's. The pupil may be pursuing a line which the teacher had not thought about or may be held back by misconceptions. Time taken listening and understanding what the pupils are saying is well spent.

(3) Being patient when the discussion seems messy and disorganized, and holding back before directing pupils.

(4) Not being afraid to challenge, tell, direct, or suggest ways forward if it seems appropriate.

(6) Helping pupils to find different ways to organize and record their patterns. Sorting, grouping and regrouping may give different ways of seeing the patterns.

(7) Encouraging a review of work in progress either in group discussion, or by using display.

(8) Extending the community by sharing classroom experiences with colleagues, either at school or through a local teachers' group (e.g. ATM[1]).

Above all, the teacher who actively encourages the plethora of patterns and relationships which can arise out of the simplest situation, and welcomes this diversity as richness rather than confusion will be more prepared for the wealth of mathematics which will be created in her classroom.

### Note

1 ATM — the Association of Teachers of Mathematics, 7 Shaftesbury Street, Derby.

# 6    Constructing Mathematics through Games

*Andrew Davis and Deirdre Pettitt*

## Introduction

The term 'game' is delightfully all-embracing. It could cover many ideas discussed earlier, such as the instances of socio-dramatic play. Any attempt to find something common to all games would probably be futile, as Wittgenstein memorably demonstrated. All we can say here is that board games and card games are the kinds of activities we especially have in mind in this chapter. We will not be discussing Monopoly, Canasta, Ludo or Bridge, but they are certainly examples of the *types* of games we want to consider.

It is scarcely original to advocate the virtues of mathematical games. So what has playing games to do with constructivism? This is a perfectly reasonable question. The answer in summary form is this. First, there are arguably aspects of games themselves which echo the socially constructed nature of mathematics. Second, if we build into our planning of game activities within the mathematics curriculum certain specified teacher roles, we then have a range of opportunities for inventing mathematics fully exemplifying our constructivist principles. Examples of such roles in classroom contexts will be developed later.

Even without a teacher role there is perhaps *something* distinctive about the intrinsic character of some games linking them closely to features of mathematics itself. This point is worth developing a little.

Our 'social constructivism' sees mathematics as embodied in the practices of human communities; there is agreement concerning the use of abstract symbols, and about how propositions expressed with such symbols relate one to another. Children are gradually initiated into these systems of rules. At the other end of the spectrum, advanced mathematicians may even create new rules, stipulate uses of new symbols, and formulate new mathematical propositions. They become increasingly aware of ways in which aspects of the rules are governed by human choices; that these features do not exist independently as absolute features of mathematics.

The use of the natural number system to count discrete items may seem wholly intuitive and unquestionable; how things must be rather than a result of human decisions. The introduction of zero, and later of negative numbers is much more obviously a matter of contingent human invention, though, needless to say hugely useful. Ideas about irrational and complex numbers take us more and more deeply into baroque abstract structures which are very obviously human creations.

Pupils are not always made aware in the mathematics classroom that rules are devised, rather than uncovered (laid down by the Deity?). It is foolish to pretend that mathematics for the majority can resemble mathematics for Einstein. At the same time, it seems unfortunate that as things are, only advanced mathematicians have a chance of becoming aware of the constructed character of the subject. Arguably we should seek ways to help ordinary pupils even at the primary school level towards at least a glimmering of such awareness.

In a good investigative activity, they may in a group context be able to decide how to use a word or a symbol, and to appreciate that given another decision, results would have been different. A well-known example would be the 3 × 3 pin board activity in which pupils are asked to discover how many different triangles can be made. Pupils can be left to decide what the term 'different' is to mean, rather than being told in advance by the teacher. Ideally, several groups will carry out the investigation with various rules for the use of 'different', and a discussion later could acknowledge the consequence of the adoption of these distinct sets of rules. One group will claim eight triangles, while another is convinced' there are more. The teacher needs to help pupils to understand that there is no question of one group being 'right' and another 'wrong'. They are simply dealing with the consequences of implementing a specific rule.

Now board games and card games involve pursuing the consequences of adopting a given set of rules. Often enough the rules are laid down for the game in question; an international body, for instance, fixes the rules of chess. Children quite naturally modify games rules to suit their own purposes; as a child I played a version of chess with friends called 'suicide chess'. This may be a conventional alternative, and I would not want to claim originality. Yet it felt to us at least, as though we had power to modify the rules, to agree on consistent implementation, and then to play through the consequences. Of course we did not have total freedom. The game had to retain an internal coherence, and enough of the rules of chess had to remain to entitle it to be thought of as a version of chess in any sense. Hence game-playing and game-modification can parallel aspects of mathematical activity.

Perhaps it is not necessary for pupils only to play *mathematical* games for these resonances between games and mathematics to be tapped, but this is a bolder claim, and we intend to restrict ourselves to mathematics in this discussion. One significant element in our games proposals will be the opportunities for students to stand back from a given set of rules, and to try the effect of altering one or more aspect of them. Ways in which this might happen are explored through several examples discussed in some detail below.

Certainly it has been fashionable for many years to advocate the use of games in school mathematics. The response from the majority of primary teachers has been muted. There have even been earnest pieces of research designed to discover whether children learn mathematics 'better' through games. (For instance, a number of such studies are discussed in Ernest, 1986). The naivety of such a research question will become apparent shortly.

The teaching roles to be discussed here often involve substantial interaction with groups of pupils. This does not imply that there is something 'wrong' with children playing games on their own. Indeed, if you know how to get groups of five to six year olds to do this without you for periods of up to 20 minutes, you could make a fortune selling this information to eager colleagues. Of course, children can gain from such activities without a teacher.

We have selected for scrutiny games chosen from a number of distinct categories. Recent typologies of games have made usefully familiar the idea that we can classify games according to their objectives. Games might:

(a)  Practise skills and help pupils to retain 'facts'.
(b)  Practise or consolidate the use of mathematical terms.
(c)  Provide opportunities for problem solving.
(d)  Help pupils to acquire new concepts. (Developed from Ernest, 1986)

Obviously this list is not complete. Nor is it suggested that a game might belong only to one category. More significantly, the classification makes no reference to the role of the teacher. How far any of these objectives are promoted would seem to depend significantly on the teacher. For instance, games ostensibly for the recall of facts could be turned by teacher and pupils in context to new purposes. Some games may lend themselves more than others to being wrenched from the designer's original objectives in the direction of new purposes, given an active teacher. With this in mind, we discuss 'drill and practice' games in addition to the more overtly investigative problem-centred games to try to indicate possibilities for 'constructivist' intervention.

A minor sub-plot of this chapter might well be the claim that recent attempts to classify maths games are deficient because they ignore the teacher, as are recent attempts to assess the effectiveness of games. This deafness to the teacher role may stem from a prevailing attitude to games which corresponds to the view of dramatic play discussed earlier; the activities are seen as less than serious, and to be done on completion of the real work. Given the potential value of games, it is strongly urged that they are built into the maths curriculum along with the other more conventional activities involving written recording. This, of course, requires careful planning, and a clear view of the concepts, processes or skills which a given game might foster when enhanced by a specific teacher role.

With this in mind, we proceed to a constructivist treatment of several kinds of games. The games are likely to be familiar to many primary teachers.

### Dominoes

These, of course, can be attempted at a huge range of levels, and are widely used for English as well as for mathematical purposes. Nursery children may be matching pictures, or pictured items up to five. Reception children may be matching pictures to numerals while top infants match small amounts of money shown in coins to amounts of money written in figures or numbers to simple calculations using any of the four operations. Juniors might attempt the matching of pictured fractions to fractions written symbolically, matching symbolic fractions to decimals, linking fractions to equivalent fractions, matching two or three digit numbers to place value illustrations employing Dienes, etc.

When children play on their own they are practising skills, perhaps of turning fractions into decimals, and at a later stage ensuring instant recall of such correspondences. Or again, they may be practising the skill of multiplying numbers, and when the game is encountered at a later stage, they are consolidating their mastery of the relevant number facts. This is fine.

Suppose the teacher sits down with a group of children who are familiar with the game. She decides to take a set of dominoes which are 'too easy' for the children, for reasons which will become apparent very shortly. So some reasonably competent Y3s might be given a set with numerals on each side . . . perhaps the numbers only go up to 20, as in Figure 6.1.

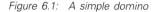

*Figure 6.1: A simple domino*

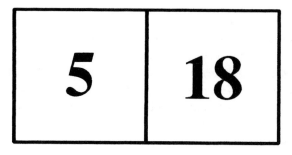

The teacher reminds her pupils that the easy (and very boring) rule for placing dominoes would be that numbers have to be the same. She asks the pupils to think of other rules. Depending on how used the pupils are to discussing their mathematics, and obviously their current grasp of basic operations, they might come up with one or more of the following:

Numbers must add up to 10.
Odd number goes with even number.
Numbers must differ by 3.
Numbers must add up to a prime number.
Numbers must add up to a number which is a multiple of 3.

The teacher might invite the pupils to decide on one of these new sets of rules and to play a couple of rounds, while she goes to attend to other children. On her return, she might ask them whether there had been any problems. Perhaps there weren't enough dominoes for the implementation of a particular rule to be practicable. The teacher invites children to suggest how the set might be extended to make the game satisfactory. Both discussion and note taking might aid the thought processes here. The children might discover on the other hand that certain rules entail that players keep having to 'knock', e.g. the prime number rule, perhaps, and that even if the set is extended an interesting game still does not result.

The point about whether children are used to working with each other and with the teacher is fundamental. It would be easy to misread the presentation of this example, and as a teacher to direct the children closely into using all the variants of the rules outlined above. As with the earlier discussion of drama and story, it is hoped that some of what is described here can actually be teased from the children; a subtle art, but one which becomes easier when both teacher and pupils have had experience of learning in this fashion.

On another occasion, the teacher might encourage children to extend the scope of new rules. What other ideas about numbers could be exploited? Their order? Perhaps the numbers form a two digit number which has to have such and such a property . . . it must be a multiple of 3, a triangular number, or whatever.

With older juniors a player might put two dominoes down at each turn, according to a rule she decides at the time. In a simple example, Sarah decides that she is forming two digit odd numbers. Hence she puts a 5 to the right of a 7, and then puts a 1 to the right of the 5, making in succession as she sees it, 75, and then 51. Debbie then places her cards according to what she deems to be the same rule. She explains her actions to Sarah and it is to be hoped that they can come to an agreement about the nature of the rule, or at least discuss the fact that more than one rule fits the 'data' on the table. Debbie might well have thought that Sarah was forming two digit numbers which were multiples of 3, and gone on to form some more of the same. Sarah might object initially, until she sees that Debbie's interpretation was perfectly legitimate in the circumstances. This is becoming quite complicated; there is scope for vigorous discussion. The teacher will be vital here. That is not to say that more able Y5s and Y6s, given the appropriately stimulating start, might not explore some of these matters at some depth before calling on an adult.

### Ladder Games

A very familiar family is outlined here, with some suggestions for new twists which might help children to think actively about the properties of the numbers concerned. (I am unable to credit any author with these games; the idea seems to be widespread.) They tend to be for juniors rather than infants, though some simple forms might work with Y2s.

For the uninitiated let us describe one moderately hard variant involving decimals (Figure 6.2). Up to four players may play. You need: 'ladders' divided into 10 spaces and a pack of cards labelled with decimals from .01 to 1 (100 cards in all).

Figure 6.2: Ladder game with decimals

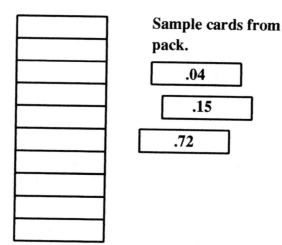

**Sample cards from pack.**

.04

.15

.72

**'ladder'.**

Each player uses his own 'ladder'. Players take turns to remove a card from the top of the pack. They then decide where to place the card on the 'ladder'. The object of the game is to end up with the decimal cards in order of magnitude, with the smallest at the bottom of the ladder and the largest at the top. As the game proceeds children may be unable to place their card on their ladder. For example, a player may have .12 and .2 immediately next to each other on his ladder, and then draw a .17 card. This needed to be placed between .12 and .2, but it cannot. Hence it is a 'dead' card, and he places it to one side. The game ends when all the cards in the pack are used up. The winner is the player with the least 'dead' cards. Alternatively, the winner is the first to complete their ladder.

As described, this is an enjoyable game which the teacher can teach the pupils, and they can then play it quite happily without further attention. They practise ordering decimals; the game could provide the teacher with a useful initial diagnostic snapshot of children's attainments if shown to a group with whom she was not yet familiar.

So far opportunities for mathematical invention are not particularly to the fore. However, suppose the teacher suggests to experienced veterans that a set of blank cards is supplied in addition to the decimal cards. If a player is in a tight corner, she may write a new decimal. Suppose she draws a card she cannot place. Then she could be allowed to write a card to suit her . . . a card which she could put somewhere else on her ladder. The rule might be that she had to use a decimal not in the pack. So if she had a space above .15, for instance, she could not write .16 if the pack itself contained all the decimals to two places from 0 to 1 which would include .16. Instead, she could be permitted to write a three place decimal . . . perhaps .154, or .156, etc. This venture would be stimulated by the teacher in discussion with the children. What other numbers could the child write to fill in remaining ladder spaces? The effect of a good discussion would be that children would 'zoom in' to a number line already expanded to show decimals, and would be helped to invent decimals which are 'in between' other numbers. Familiar issues concerning the way the place value system is extended to cover decimals would be re-explored.

In an easier guise, ladder games ask players to order whole numbers from a pack provided with numbers from 1 to 100. Again, veterans could be encouraged to write themselves out of difficult situations, the rule once more being that they could not use numbers in the pack. They would be encouraged to come up with fractions, or decimals, or even to choose either.

A challenging version of the game contains a mixture of fractions, decimals and percentages, representing numbers in these three ways from .01 through to 1, with only one of each number. So, for example, if a half occurs in the pack as 50 per cent, it does not also figure as .5 or ½. Or if a quarter is represented in the pack as ¼ then it does not also appear as 0.25 or 25 per cent. This requires pupils to be around level 5–6 in National Curriculum terms. They could be challenged to write extra cards in decimal form if otherwise they would be unable to play a card to their ladder. Undoubtedly the opportunity to create new cards to escape from difficult situations in a sense undermines the game-like quality of the activity, but this need not affect either motivation or mathematical interest.

### Place Value Game: Numero

One more brief example concludes this section, and again it has no pretensions to novelty. Two children, A and B armed with paper and pencil are supplied with a pack of cards marked with numerals 0 to 9. Only one of each numeral is supplied.

They draw on the paper two sets of three boxes, as in Figure 6.3; these will eventually become two three-digit numbers. A's objective in the game is to make a three digit number larger than B's, and vice versa. They take it in turns to draw a card. They may decide whether to write the number in one of their squares, or in one of their opponent's

Figure 6.3

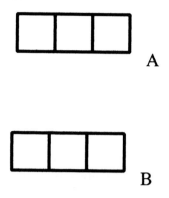

A

B

squares. When a card has been used, it is placed at the bottom of the pack. When six cards have been drawn, the winner may be determined, though often it is obvious well before the end.

Those who have used this with Y2s, Y3s or Y4s over the years will testify to the children's enjoyment of it. Clearly it provides practice of place value, gives the teacher who uses it with a new group the opportunity to make a first step into diagnosing place value problems, and informal ideas about probability may also be encouraged. The objective of making the larger three digit number may be varied. Four digit numbers could be tried, or decimals, etc.

After reasonably extensive experience of the game, the teacher may venture with Y3s and Y4s at least into some discussion. Which numbers do they like drawing early in the game? Why? Which numbers are difficult to decide about? Why? So far, this is fairly obvious, and what most teachers would do quite naturally at some stage without giving the matter much thought. By way of putting more control into the hands of the pupils, the cheater's fantasies might be made legitimate. Suppose, the teacher suggests to a group, you were able to organize the order in which the cards came up, rather than a decently random sequence being available from an efficient card shuffle. First of all, how could you fix it for the first player to win with a given objective? Or the second player? How could you make life as difficult as possible for both of them? Once you have recorded your cheater's charter, find some willing victims who can test your theories.

Things can become quite interesting if you make the objectives a little more esoteric, as Dave Kirkby suggests in some of his booklets on these games (Kirkby, 1983). The aim might be to reach the nearest three digit number to 501, and to prevent your partner from getting as near as you. Other possibilities might be to try to get a prime number and to stop your partner from so doing, etc. Organizing the card pack to help one player rather than the other to win might take some thought. The game might be widened to allow for three players, with nine boxes to fill. On any one turn, a player can write in one of his own boxes, or in a box belonging to one of his two opponents. In the spirit of earlier activities described in this book, it would be nice to have a session with the children in which experienced players come up with fresh rules, and these can be tested out.

### Inventing Mathematics Through Games: Relying less on the Teacher

As noted earlier, there is nothing 'wrong' with children playing games on their own. Apart from the evident difficulties of organization, the task for teachers may be to ensure that children do so as profitably as possible. It has to be accepted that teachers cannot be everywhere at once so, having accepted that maximum benefit occurs when teachers can work with children to guide their inventions, we can look at how teachers working with children can spill over into self-selected and directed activities. A first point is that, because they have played games with teachers, children know that these activities are valued in the classroom.

Children often play cards and other mathematical games outside of school, learning some mathematics painlessly and enjoyably. In school enjoyment continues. However, it seems necessary to us that children should also be aware that they are learning mathematics. Children understand that school has serious purposes. They tend to object to activities that they don't regard as their 'work' which more often than not in their view, is the commercial mathematics scheme (Desforges and Cockburn, 1989). So, if games children play without the teacher are to hold children's interest they need to be seen as part of the mathematics curriculum, not just as things to do when work has been completed. Furthermore, because children have been made familiar with games they have some understanding of rules and constraints, know how to alter rules with common agreement, know that new strategies can be invented and realize that it is necessary to think ahead. The classroom ethos, in short, is permeated by the broad constructivist principles we advocate.

Teachers also have a crucial role in setting up games for children to play without them, starting, of course, with how to play. They also select, and encourage children to play those games which are likely to be of most value to any particular group. This requires awareness of attainment and concepts which will match or challenge that attainment. A good many games played without the teacher will be practice. Practice is essential and a number game can provide many more sums in the same period of time than when worksheets are used. However, children will not benefit from practising skills which they already have. Once calculation has become automatic and fast no further benefit is available unless the game is made more challenging or there is a possibility of higher order invention through practice of lower order skills. This is possible if, for example, the need to get a little quicker causes children to count on, instead of counting all from one. Teachers have to be aware of ceilings and possibilities in the selection of games.

From time to time teachers will also have to observe children who are working without them. They have to check their hunches and the operation of the game. In addition, of course, children absorbed in a game offer a splendid opportunity for informal and unobtrusive assessment. Teachers will also be checking how the social groupings they have set up work in practice. Groups can be constituted by friendship, attainment, mixed attainment or randomly (always bearing in mind that the game should be broadly appropriate to learning). It seems sensible to have higher attainers working with lower attainers. Often this benefits both groups. However, if this is to work higher attainers also have to be kind and patient, not only about mathematics but also about fumbled shuffling or wild guesses or general slowness. Not all children are helpful to 'slowcoaches'. Adults can learn from hard taskmasters. One of the authors improved rapidly at cribbage when her partner deducted her uncounted points from her score. Whether children can cope with this sort of thing lies within the judgment of the teacher. Teachers will also be watching to see when a game has to be withdrawn or extended.

The character of the rules of a game also needs monitoring. Unless players are very evenly matched the rules should ensure that each player has a turn where he or she has a chance to think. That is, the rules should not be like snap where the quickest child wins every time. Ideally there should also be opportunities built into a game for every child to attend to others turns as well as their own.

The game which follows can and has been played by children as young as top Reception. It has been selected because it has been found to enable children not only to practise existing counting skills but also to invent basic addition and to begin to look for complex patterns in how numbers are constituted. They do this for themselves or by observing other players. The game is called Make 5 but can be adapted to use any suitable number.

### Make Five

*Materials*: 36 cards, 6 numbered 0, 6 numbered 1, 6 numbered 2, 6 numbered 3, 6 numbered 4, 6 numbered 5
*Number of players*: 3
*Method*: Cards are shuffled and dealt out face down to each player. In turn, each player turns a card face up next to his or her pile. The player who has turned a card over may collect all the cards which are face up which total 5, e.g. 3 and 2. The cards collected are kept separately by each child and the winner has the most cards when they have been exhausted.
*What children learn*: To start with children look for the obvious pairs like 2 and 3. Before long they will notice that zero can be involved, e.g. 5 and 0 and that more than two numbers can be collected, e.g. 2 and 2 and 1. The child waiting for his or her turn is likely to begin to predict, e.g. 'I need a 2'. This means that the child is dealing with

$3 + x = 5$

which baffles many children. It will probably still baffle them in its early written notation, which is normally expressed as

$3 + \text{'}\square\text{'} = 5$

Transfer from practical work to written notation is at least as hard as transfer from written work to use and application. If teachers at some point observe that children are comfortable with the idea of 'how many more needed' there is an opportunity to intervene, suggest that children record their scores and help them to do so. The connection between the sums and the notation may thereby be established.

### Notes on 'Make Five'

A rule needs to be established that only the top exposed cards are taken into account. Otherwise, a child might take a 3 from an exposed pile and note that the card underneath was zero and take that too. Cards which are not collected after a 5 is made can be returned to the bottom of the owner's pile. It is important that only the child whose turn it is collects a five if there is one. It is worth repeating that this gives a child a chance to think and others a chance to make suggestions.

We turn now to some practical issues.

## Designing and Making Materials for a Game

There is no reason not to use and especially adapt games which are commercially available. Sometimes these are rather too ornate and children are attracted to the decorations not the mathematics. More importantly the claims for the concepts which can be learned are occasionally dubious. Any game where counters are moved round a track involves counting but not as can be claimed, counting on. (That is, if your counter is on 5 and you throw 3, you count 1,2,3 not 6,7,8.) Indeed, for the youngest children it is preferable not to number spaces at all. This only confuses counting. Sometimes commercial games do not have a start which is not on the track. This is needed, otherwise children start to count on the track, i.e. at 2, which is not the way to introduce children to a counting track. A respected mathematics scheme even numbers the first space on a track as zero which is confusing. So, use such games but do not assume that because they are published they are beyond criticism.

Making one's own games is not difficult. It is essential to try out any new idea with children before you expend time and effort with felt tips and sticky transparent protection. See if it works and teaches the concepts you have identified and then make a more permanent item. You can tell children that your first attempt may need revision and have them comment and make suggestions.

## What Sorts of Things Attract Children or Put Them Off?

Your prototypes will not put children off. They tend to be more interested in the game than the presentation. They especially enjoy any game where items can be collected. These can be coins, of course, or Christmas cracker snaps or any tiny toys or bits of sparkly broken jewellery. Exchange games also benefit from interesting items to swap and counters for moves are liked more and are more easily identified if they are not just coloured disks. (Remember five green houses for a red hotel and the flat iron and the battleship in Monopoly?) Younger children tend to prefer short games and will play a short game several times more eagerly than one long one.

Games frequently contain a competitive element. Most children do not seem to be over competitive or worry too much if they do not win.

If a game is played several times, of course, there is more chance of winners being spread. Children like to finish, i.e. in a track game each child coming second or third will often say 'Now I've won'. The negotiations such as 'whose turn is it?' can become minor quarrels but sometimes children seem to prefer these negotiations to playing with a computer which brooks no argument. Frequently the order in which children decide to take turns seems odd. Often it is not the expected clockwise direction but goes backwards and forward across players. However, children are rather good at remembering an order which they established. Overall, children like games and are unlikely to have to be dragged from 'work' in their books if they also know that these games make them better at mathematics.

### Other Practical Matters

How games will be stored and will be available to teachers and children need to be thought through, often at the design stage. Each game needs to have its own box or folder to which is firmly affixed:

(a)   The concepts and the level of each concept which the game may teach, e.g. 'addition within 20'.
(b)   The materials in a list so children can check these before and after a game.
(c)   How to play.

Instructions to be read and written are important to the English curriculum as well as to mathematics. Children can be asked to make their own games, which is a logical extension to playing and tests their mathematics. They will also learn how hard it is to explain what is clear to you, to others. If a game is extended, for example changing counting to addition by using two dice it is probably best to make it again and put it in a fresh container. Otherwise instructions get very muddled and complex. Of course, children can be encouraged to use their own extensions and constraints when playing an existing game. 'How can you make it harder?' is sensible if easy-peasy is the complaint.

## Conclusion

Games which children play by themselves are almost invariably more limited in scope and application than those where teachers are involved.

However, like those games they provide the necessity to use and apply mathematics and to extend skills, strategies and cognition. Often it is not until this need arises that children see mathematics in school as more than getting the answers right in their books. Games are perhaps the easiest and most direct link or bridge between pencil and paper activities and what you can do with these skills.

# 7    The World of Sounds and Mathematical Construction

*Andrew Davis*

## Introduction

On the whole just two of our five senses are made use of by children learning mathematics at Key Stages 1 and 2, namely sight and touch. This chapter explores the thought that we might extend that number to three, and include hearing. (This idea was touched on, of course, by Maria Goulding in chapter 5.) It should be acknowledged at the outset that there is no intrinsic link between constructivism and the idea that we might make more use of sounds within primary mathematics. However, the idea has the advantage of novelty. We have an excuse to explore some more unusual activities while at the same time illustrating further the basic principles for teaching and learning mathematics defended in chapter 2.

Consider first some broad considerations in favour of employing sounds during the first stages of learning mathematics. The senses of sight and touch play a very significant role in early number curricula. Young children sort objects according to colour and shape. They are shown small sets of objects and taught to count them. When the child has had plenty of experience with physical objects, whether commercially produced or natural, they are invariably presented with work sheets or cards for practice and consolidation.

One common assumption is that the stage of illustrations on such sheets or cards, is a stepping stone on the way to abstract understanding. Teachers and the producers of commercial schemes seem to agree on this. Pictures of elephants to be counted, are one step away from the physical reality of live creatures, and one small step towards context free numbers. The two-dimensional diagrams of Dienes apparatus — the depiction of hundreds, tens and units, are thought to move the child away from the necessity of handling wooden or plastic apparatus, and towards a stage where computations can be performed without the benefit of pictures or materials.

Even more significantly, we have a tendency to use this half-way house notation in the ways in which we require the children to respond. In their answers, the children may be expected to draw so many elephants or to 'match the members of one set with the members of another by drawing lines between them.' They may be asked to draw quasi-Dienes pictures of the tens and units of which such and such a number is constituted. Again, these visual numbers are thought to be less abstract than answers which merely use symbols; they are supposed to be closer to the experiences of physical objects than the corresponding number sentences in symbolic form.

This is not the place to review research into the role of materials (and by implication, pictures of materials) in fostering the growth of key mathematical concepts. As a matter of fact research evidence suggests that many children do not readily transfer from operating with physical objects to abstract thinking, even in the context of carefully structured programmes which seemingly make good use of relevant equipment (see, for example Johnson, 1989). However, we assume here that we need to improve the quality of learning sequences in which materials play an important role, rather than to abandon such practical work in the face of the mixed messages stemming from this research.

Given this assumption, this chapter contends that there should be occasions when the child is expected to hear and to produce sounds in the context of a mathematical problem, rather than demonstrating something with physical objects or drawing, reading or writing. The proposal is meant to be a modest one: evidently there would be formidable practical problems with a wholesale auditory maths curriculum! Numbers should be kept small. Using sounds is constrained by short-term memory limitations. I can see thirteen ducks on the page, and if I forget how many there are or count them incorrectly, I can count them again. If I hear thirteen sounds, they are gone and I cannot repair any mistakes or check my memory.

Good infant teachers have always known that for a substantial majority of their pupils, you need at least twenty ways of presenting the idea before the children begin to grasp it. You have to present the idea in a variety of contexts, using a range of apparatus, with a diversity of language. Key Stage 1 teachers have long understood, to put this point another way, what it is to 'know' a mathematical proposition; some time was spent in chapter 2 in unpacking this elusive idea. 'Knowing' entails being able to apply what is known in an indefinitely large number of diverse circumstances.

Possibly a minority of children will find it *easier* to learn from sounds than from pictures. One obvious set of candidates would be visually impaired children. However, there is very little in the literature about any work being done of this kind for such pupils. Any readers who know of any might be kind enough to let us know!

Low attaining juniors — Y3s and Y4s — need something new to revive their flagging motivation in matters of basic counting. They have exhausted the average teacher's repertoire, and often associate typical materials with the Key Stage 1 classes to which they are very anxious to feel superior. Activities with sounds may well strike these children as novel, even if they are in the last analysis a mundane reworking of simple number ideas.

Where sounds are being counted, or where sounds and movements are being coordinated, we have on the face of it excellent contexts for promoting early counting and matching which rival the more conventional processes involving physical objects. For instance, in a case of simple matching, the teacher might sound three on a tambourine. Children would respond with the same number of sounds on their instrument. The subtle difference between this process, and processes of 'matching' using objects, is that pupils have to count, and *remember*. They then construct a matching set of sounds.

In work leading up to addition and subtraction, the teacher sounds out, say four. The child is asked to respond with one *more*. The child has to *remember*, and then go on one, so as to give five in total. Children might practise building up numbers. A row of children might have instruments: each one might be required to do one more than the previous one. Or the opposite. Begin with, say five. Then each child might be asked to do one less than the one before, until zero is reached.

Using sounds might be a device for strongly encouraging the 'count-on' method of adding. For instance, the teacher is working with the children on adding 7 and 3. The children up to now have persisted in counting up *all* the numbers . . . 1, 2, 3, 4, 5, 6, 7 . . . 8, 9, 10. The teacher might announce that she is going to make 7 sounds, and then 3 sounds, and that she wants the children to help her discover the total. Accordingly, she sounds 7. The 7 have now 'gone'. When she sounds out three more, the children will be compelled to 'go on' from 7, and say 8, 9, 10 as the new sounds are produced.

These very basic activities seem to link with the 'auditory patterning' recommended by Carol Thornton (Thornton, C., 1989).

> Clap one, two or three times and ask students to tell how many claps they heard . . .

Close your eyes while I bounce the ball. How many bounces do
you hear?

Or the activity might be introduced during a music period to the
beat of a drum or a tambourine.

When children become comfortable with this activity, she suggests that
the teacher proceed to the following:

How many numbers do you hear? Say two or three numbers in
sequence (forward or backward) and ask students to tell how many
numbers they heard, for example:

'Six, seven, eight' (Three numbers)

'Ten, nine' (Two numbers)

Given 5 + 3, for example, she observed that her students tended to
recognize (without finger counting) when they had counted on three
more:

'FIVE-six, seven, eight'.

## Examples with a Constructivist Flavour

So much then, for general justifications and exemplifications of the role
of sounds in mathematics learning. Constructivist principles have not
been explicitly addressed. We now move to a consideration of a range
of classroom activities where, as in previous chapters, the suggested
interactions between pupils, between teachers and pupils, and the location of the control of the processes is more explicitly constructivist.

Before proceeding, we need to make one or two practical points.
Some of the following ideas need 'sound dice'. A tape recorder or
computer is set up to produce random groups of sounds, which may
mimic ordinary dice, but frequently are idiosyncratic . . . details will be
given later when we elaborate the activities. The ideal mechanism for
these in the 1990s is the computer. It is easier to control. A tape recorder may be used with quite young children, but it has to be switched
off after a given group of sounds. However, with careful training at the
beginning, five and six year olds can manage perfectly well. For those
with simple programming skills, it would be straightforward to program
the computer in the corner of your classroom to produce groups of
sounds in the way required.

Several ideas are elaborated in some detail in the remaining part of the main chapter, with explicit attention given to 'constructivist' developments. A number of other sound activities are appended at the end of this chapter. The constructivist slant on these is not comprehensively spelled out; we hope that the discerning reader can by then select and transform according to whatever constructivist leanings he or she may have acquired.

### Fletcher Games with Sound Dice

These are auditory versions of games for Reception children found in the old Fletcher scheme resource book. Just one example is outlined here. The games promote very simple counting and matching. The game is best played with two or three children so that individual children do not need to wait long for their turn.

Prepare a cassette with clearly separated groups of sounds, paced so they can be counted by young children. Sometimes there will be three sounds in a group, and sometimes four. Ensure that it is a matter of chance which it is. Or provide a computer programme to produce similar sounds. Also create a game worksheet with pictures of stools without legs on which children can draw, or similar boards, with cut-out 'legs' which may be placed under the stool seats.

*Figure 7.1: Stools game*

The game proceeds as follows: the cassette has groups of sounds . . . either fours, or threes, with clear spaces between each group. Use this as a 'sound dice'. Or the computer, on pressing the space bar, will produce either four sounds, or three. Whether a given group of sounds is a 'four' or a 'three' is entirely random.

Each child has a paper or board of legless stools (the first stool is drawn with legs to show that three are required for a completed stool). Children take turns to listen and count a group of sounds, switching off the recorder when their sounds have finished. If four sounds are heard, the child does nothing. If three are heard, the child draws in three legs. The first child to complete a row of stools wins.

With an adult present, all the children might be encouraged to count and match the sounds as they are heard, by saying the number words, and putting out a unifix block or multilink for each sound. Alternatively, stool legs can be put out from a central stock; pupils can then compare the result with the completed stool on their board, and decide whether they may put legs on another stool. When children have grown accustomed to the dice, a 'constructivist' development might consist of a blindfolded child armed with a drum who would take over the function of the dice. She would decide whether to beat three, or another number. In contrast to the work with the tape or computer sequence, there could be a choice about what the number was to be when it was not the special number three. The control of the activities would be shifted towards the children. Pupils would be choosing numbers they felt able to cope with.

Children could later be encouraged to suggest other objects to figure on new game boards . . . dolls, spiders, beetles, etc., and to work out what kind of dice would be suitable for such games. Evidently discussion with an adult would be crucial: these ideas would not emerge full-blown from a typical group of reception children! If they were involved in creating the boards, they would need to ensure that each board contained the same number of objects, and that the first object had the appropriate number of legs, buttons, windows or whatever. There could be many opportunities for pupils to make choices, building on their existing mathematical understanding, with appropriate interventions from the skilled teacher.

### Beginnings of Algebra: Pattern Making in Sound

The following activities can begin with Reception children, and appropriately extended in complexity to suit Y1 and Y2 pupils. The relevant National Curriculum programme of study is level 1 of Attainment Target 3:

Copying, continuing and devising repeating patterns represented by objects/apparatus or single digit numbers.

Have available any small set of contrasting instruments. (However, claps, voice sounds, whispers, etc. could easily be used instead.) The teacher sounds out a simple sequence, e.g. xylophone, xylophone, tambourine, xylophone, xylophone, tambourine, xylophone, xylophone, tambourine. The children are first asked to copy the pattern. After some practice, they could be encouraged to continue it also.

Next, children can be encouraged to create their own sequence and repeat it. They may have to be restrained from making matters too complicated! Some children may need to spend plenty of time at this stage. Friends could be invited to make specific movements to correspond with the sounds . . . a jump for the tambourine, and a crouch for the xylophone. Sometimes the movement sequences could be composed first, and then the sound pattern constructed to correspond with these.

At a later stage, the teacher could begin to encourage the use of symbol notation, e.g. associating a simple shape or colour with a particular noise. For example, square = tambourine beat; triangle = triangle beat; circle = chime bar. The children would draw, or place prepared symbols from left to right (itself a very useful feature for a range of Key Stage 1 pupils).

They could then compose their own patterns, and record in this simple notation. Other children could 'play' from the 'score'. In the hall, again movements could be associated with particular sounds, to produce repeating patterns of activity . . . jump, jump, skip, jump, jump, skip, etc. Children working in twos or threes could be challenged to see how many different patterns could be produced from two or three sound types.

Advanced developments might focus rather more on the numbers of sounds concerned. Associated ideas involving rhythm are mentioned in a separate sketch below.

### *'Playing Turtle' Using Sound Commands*

One child takes on the role of 'turtle', i.e. the device driven by LOGO type commands. One or more associates may issue commands to the child pretending to be the device which she obeys implicitly. Commands could include FORWARD n (meaning that the turtle must take n steps forward, BACK n (meaning that the turtle takes n steps back), LEFT (turn a quarter of a turn (90 degrees) to the left), and RIGHT means a quarter of a turn to the right.

The 'master' could have three musical instruments with which to issue commands.

Perhaps a drum or tambourine for the number of STEPS to be taken.

Perhaps a low chime bar note for LEFT.
A high chime bar note for RIGHT.

The 'master' can attempt to steer turtle to a particular objective, round furniture, through a large maze made from boxes/painted on large sheets of paper placed on the floor, etc. The turtle's job is to listen carefully to the sounds, and move accordingly.

Young children and low attainers would need to take the activity in very small chunks at a time. That is to say, the sounds for steps would be issued, for instance, and the turtle would execute these immediately, before any new sound commands were forthcoming. Older and more experienced children may be able to execute short command sequences after hearing them. The 'master' may need pencil and paper on which to plan his commands.

The turtle might systematically malfunction, e.g. always take two more steps than those asked for. This kind of suggestion would be introduced by the teacher, and systematically practised by the children before they were sent away to try out variants on their own. The activity then turns into a 'guess my rule' process with a slightly unusual format. After teacher initiation, the direction of activity would gradually be given into the hands of the pupils. The capacity to formulate a coherent malfunction, and to manifest it consistently, would be a key development on the part of the child. Certain kinds of attempts would force children to stretch their ideas. What should be done if the malfunction is to take two less steps than those asked for, and the master commands one step forward? Would it be logical to take one step backwards? Perhaps malfunctions could be planned by pairs of children, and this thorny issue could be debated before a decision was implemented.

### Guess My Rule: Sound Version

This is the old 'function machine' activity, using sounds. It belongs nicely with the turtle activity above, if the latter is developed to include the malfunction idea.

It should be played with a small group of children, each of whom has a musical instrument of some kind. Child X, who has a drum, thinks of a simple rule, e.g. 'add two'. Other children take turns to use their instruments to sound out numbers. For example, someone plays five notes on a chime bar. X responds with seven beats on the drum. Children keep trying numbers on X, until they guess from X's responses what the 'rule' is. The rules can vary in complexity, depending on the attainment of the children, though for practical reasons the numbers need to be kept fairly small.

The activity may be reversed initially, to help low attainers into this activity. Again, each child in a small group is given a musical instrument. A function is announced by a leader, e.g. ADD three. The leader then taps out a number of his choice under ten e.g. four. He points to someone in the group, who must tap out four, plus three more. The rest of the group count, and check that it is correct.

Constructivist elements can come to the fore in discussions and extensions with children after plenty of initial experience at the practical level. These developments are more likely at Key Stage 2. Once a particular rule is understood, the rule creator might be encouraged to challenge others with suggestions such as: 'Make me give you seven' (or any other suitable number), and the challenge is met by producing the appropriate number of sounds to stimulate the 'output' of seven mentioned to start with.

Perish the thought that anyone would cheat by changing their rule when the guesses become uncomfortably successful. Yet pupils *could* be asked to think about ways in which a potential cheat could be required to record their rule. This recording would be done by the potential cheat before processing other pupils' numbers so that they could guess the rule in question. Probably simple use of basic operators . . . (+4) (×2 +3) might suffice. Such representations would correspond to primitive symbolic algebraic sentences. The children would be making written records of simple functions. Useful interchanges on the precedence of operators might occur. It would be natural to operate on numbers in the order from left to right in which the sentence was written. 'Arithmetical' calculators of the kind pupils would be likely to encounter in the primary school do just that, whereas scientific calculators behave otherwise. At Y5/6 level this might be explored with some pupils. The sound stimulus at this stage is fading in importance, and could become a positive nuisance if larger numbers were needed. It should be abandoned when necessary.

### 'Musical' Versions of FIZZ-BUZZ

This is suitable for children who understand the idea of multiples and factors, and are working on their tables. In its simplest form, it should work with some Y2s, and in more advanced guise will suit a range of Key Stage 2 pupils.

Two children, A and B are each supplied with an instrument, of contrasting types. They are also each assigned a multiplication table.

Suppose one child with a xylophone is given 2, and a second child with a tambourine is given 3. A leader takes a drum, to 'keep the beat'. She sounds this slowly and regularly. The class begins to count the drum beats, beginning with 1. As counting proceeds, the '2' child must look out for multiples of 2, and sound her xylophone for each one, i.e. on 2, 4, 6 . . . ; similarly the '3' child must look out for multiples of 3 and bang her tambourine accordingly. The *same* activity focusing on the *same* multiples needs to be repeated several times, and children can then begin to sense a kind of rhythm to the patterns created. Children may previously have coloured in multiples of 2, and of 3 on 100 squares. These could be available initially for reference, as in Figure 7.2.

*Figure 7.2: Multiples of 2*

| 1 | 2 | 3 | 4 | 5 | 6 | 7 | 8 | 9 | 10 |
|---|---|---|---|---|---|---|---|---|---|
| 11 | 12 | 13 | 14 | 15 | 16 | 17 | 18 | 19 | 20 |
| 21 | 22 | 23 | 24 | 25 | 26 | 27 | 28 | 29 | 30 |
| 31 | 32 | 33 | 34 | 35 | 36 | 37 | 38 | 39 | 40 |
| 41 | 42 | 43 | 44 | 45 | 46 | 47 | 48 | 49 | 50 |
| 51 | 52 | 53 | 54 | 55 | 56 | 57 | 58 | 59 | 60 |
| 61 | 62 | 63 | 64 | 65 | 66 | 67 | 68 | 69 | 70 |
| 71 | 72 | 73 | 74 | 75 | 76 | 77 | 78 | 79 | 80 |
| 81 | 82 | 83 | 84 | 85 | 86 | 87 | 88 | 89 | 90 |
| 91 | 92 | 93 | 94 | 95 | 96 | 97 | 98 | 99 | 100 |

Try a similar activity for other numbers, and/or three numbers. Younger or less able children could try the activity concentrating on *one* multiplication table only, at least to start with.

The obvious discussion points are numbers where more than one instrument must be sounded. Children could predict from a given point in the counting sequence when the next coincidence would occur, and so on. Moves to stimulate children's 'construction' might include inverting the activity so that numbers which are *not* multiples of n are picked out by instruments. Or the counting could be reversed. After plenty of practice, as was indicated above, children become familiar with the rhythm of the patterns created. At this stage, a child could listen with eyes closed while instrumentalists pick up the pattern from an arbitrary point . . . say 11. No counting would be done. After continuing the pattern for a while, the listener could be invited to guess from which number the instrumentalists had started. Repeats would be necessary before intelligent guesses could be made. Depending on which tables were being used, more than one correct answer would be possible. In discussion, the various possibilities could be explored.

### Rhythm and Number

For Y2s and some lower attaining Y3s, Y4s (?) who have, or could be helped to acquire a sense of rhythm. The activity would follow very naturally on from work on repeating patterns described above, and could help children to develop early ideas about multiples.

First, children need to experience and to produce rhythm patterns. For example, triple time . . . ONE two three, ONE two three. Or quadruple time . . . ONE two three four, ONE two three four. They could practise moving to such rhythms in the hall. Perhaps a small group might produce the sounds on percussion. Again, the percussion group must practise producing the rhythms. Many children would need a number of brief rehearsals over a period of several weeks before they were confident and competent.

A percussion group can then compose 'tunes' made from complete bars. For example, working in triple time only using two instruments, a bar might consist of a tambourine for the first beat, and chime bars for second and third beats, thus:

TAMBOURINE   CHIME   CHIME

A 'master counter' should be appointed to count the total number of notes produced. Thus, e.g. when a tune in triple time gets under way, the counter will say:

'ONE   two   three   FOUR   five   six   SEVEN   eight   nine   TEN   eleven   twelve.'

for a 'tune' twelve notes long in triple time.

Obviously this task will be easier if the first beat in each bar is emphasized and played with a distinctive instrument. Children have to practise the rhythms and the counting so they can carry them out in a coordinated fashion.

A group of children could then be asked to generate as many tunes of differing lengths in triple time using complete bars as they could think of. Total numbers of notes could be restricted to, say 36. They should record the total number of notes used in each tune. Similar tasks can be given for duple time and quadruple time. (While music sometimes is written with five beats in a bar, this is not an 'easy' rhythm, and is not recommended.)

It may be appropriate to encourage children to devise a simple notation for recording their 'compositions'. This would help them to keep track of the number of bars played, and links could then be made with simple multiplications. Later, discuss with children which numbers over four never represent the total numbers of notes in 'compositions'. (Another route into the idea of prime numbers.)


### Symmetrical Compositions

This activity should suit some Y5s and Y6s, and assumes a solid grounding in mirror symmetry.

*(a) Non-pitched version.*  Children armed with instruments create a short tune of, say four or five notes, e.g.

DRUM   DRUM   chime   bar   triangle   wood block

The 'answering phrase' is to be composed by another group, which must precisely mirror the initial theme:

wood   block   triangle   chime bar   DRUM   DRUM

The first half is then played, followed immediately by the second half, to provide the symmetrical composition. Obviously the teacher would introduce this gently, with a number of examples using very short tunes.

Children might adopt some method of notation, and this would, of course, reveal the symmetry in a visual fashion. Try not to resort to this too soon. Encourage children to hear the symmetry in the answering half. If necessary, introduce the principle with very simple tunes . . . only two or three notes long.

In a development, note *length* could also be varied. One advantage of this activity is that it shows up the problems with the term 'same' when we tell children that a shape with line symmetry is the 'same' each side of the line of symmetry. Arguably if the tune is simply *repeated* we have the most obvious use of the term 'same'. An analogy would be a straightforward translation of a plane shape. In the symmetry context, the meaning of 'same' is enriched. The idea is that activities of the kind described here help pupils to construct this richer meaning.

*(b) Pitched version.* Use tuned percussion . . . xylophone, glockenspiel, chime bars. Activity basically as in (a). For example, decide that the tune will employ a particular 'low' note, one of 'middle' pitch, and also one of 'high' pitch. The first half of a 'tune' might consist of:

LOW   LOW   HIGH   MIDDLE   HIGH

Hence the second half must be:

HIGH   MIDDLE   HIGH   LOW   LOW

Again, children might be encouraged to record their 'compositions' using some form of notation.

Key Stage 2 children who can read music could record the pitched version in traditional form. More able children could work more carefully on the melodic aspect of each half, and be encouraged to discover melodies which sound pleasing 'either way round'. (J.S. Bach experimented with devices of this kind, e.g. in 'The Art of Fugue.')

### Further Activities

*Slippery Slope Game* (Adapted from Richard Skemp)

*You need*: 'Slippery slope' board as shown in Figure 7.3. Three pairs of tokens, e.g. two blues, two reds, two greens. 'Auditory dice' from computer or tape recorder.
The board represents steps up a hillside. Steps 11, 12 and 13 are missing. Here there is a slippery slope, and if a climber treads here she slides back to a lower step as shown by the arrows. The object is to reach the top.

Each player manages two 'climbers'. Players in turn count a group of pips from the sound dice, and move one of their climbers that number of steps up. They begin at START, which corresponds to zero. A climber may not move up to a step which is already occupied. Overtaking is allowed.

*Figure 7.3:  Slippery Slope Game (Skemp, 1989)*

Players may choose not to move. However, if a climber has been touched, it must be moved. If a climber is touched, and the move would take her to an occupied step, she must return to the start. The exact number must be thrown to finish.

(The use of a 'sound dice' means that children do not have a visible die in front of them to check and recheck the number they are entitled to move. Perhaps each player could be encouraged to count and check the 'pips' for the person whose turn it is, and to keep a running record of numbers as they come up in sounds.)

Skemp would not talk in constructivist terms; nevertheless, the game is designed to force children to think mentally about where on the number line certain moves would take them. They are discouraged from touching a 'climber' and moving until they have properly thought through all the moves. Interestingly this is in effect extending the constructivist idea explored comprehensively elsewhere in this book. It is now being taken to include some types of imaginative efforts, which may assist the learner to build and invent new structures on the basis of what she already knows.

*Stepping Stone Game* (Loosely related to an idea by Richard Skemp)

*You need*: 'Stepping Stone' board as shown in Figure 7.4. Three tokens. 'Auditory dice' from computer or tape recorder.

*Figure 7.4:  Stepping Stone Game*

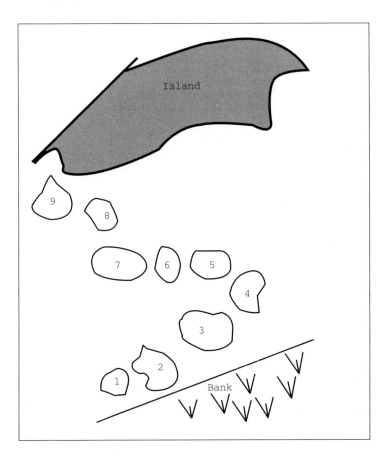

*Rules*: (these have been changed from Skemp's in one or two important respects).

A game for 2 or 3 players. Probably Y1.

Players take turns to use the sound dice. They begin with their tokens on the bank, which represents zero. They move the number of stones indicated by their group of pips. BUT, they may choose whether to go (but once they have touched their player, or the board, they must move). If a player's move takes him to the same stone as another player, he knocks them into the stream, and they return to the start. Stone 5 is wobbly. Any player who lands on it falls in the stream and returns to the bank. The 'constructivist' principle here again is the peculiar framing of the rules, which force players to construct a number line in their heads so to speak before finally committing themselves to a move.

(The use of a 'sound dice' means that children do not have a visible die in front of them to check and re-check the number they are entitled to move. Perhaps each player could be encouraged to count and check the 'pips' for the person whose turn it is, and to keep a running record of numbers as they come up in sounds. Young children might make tally marks for each pip heard.)

It would be important for the teacher to hold short discussions with players once they were familiar with the basic rules. During a game, the children could be encouraged to think out loud about where their dice throw would take them were they to move, and whether in consequence they actually wish to move.

### Ways of Making Nine

For individual children, or pairs. Y1, Y2 and some low achieving juniors. *You need*: a tape or computer programme to produce many examples of 'making nine' in different ways using contrasting sounds, e.g.:

3 high sounds, 6 low sounds.
1 high sound, 8 low sounds,
etc.

Each way of making nine would separated from the next on a tape by a clear space.

Children might have accompanying worksheets. They could keep a tally of the high sounds heard, and of the low sounds. Some might be at a stage where they could appropriately be asked to complete a relevant addition sentence in symbol form.

On some occasions the child will hear NO high sounds, and nine low sounds, in which case they should be writing:

**0 + 9 = 9**

Similarly they may hear nine high sounds followed by NO low sounds, in which case they should end up writing:

**9 + 0 = 9**

Obviously if this was felt to be too difficult for given pupils, the 'zero options' could be omitted from the tape sequence.

The worksheet method of recording is far from exciting. Children instead might be encouraged to build a tower from bricks, with a 'high' place and a 'low' place on which figures could be stood. They could be asked to count out nine figures at the start. These figures could be placed high on the tower for a high sound, and low down for a low sound, etc.

In a given period of time, it might well be that not all the combinations for making nine would come up. Children could be encouraged to think of the remaining possibilities. In order that they begin to pick up on the idea of *exhausting* the possibilities, referred to by Woodhouse in chapter 4, some kind of systematic recording might be suggested if they are capable of working at this level.

# 8    Children Drawing

*Jennifer Buckham*

## Introduction

> Since it is not generally appreciated that mathematics is embedded within art, it does seem worthwhile to explicate and highlight these aspects. In doing so we may not only deepen our understanding of mathematics, but also heighten our perception of art (Matthews, 1991).

The purpose of this chapter is to explore the relationship between mathematics and art, highlighting in particular the potentially rich opportunities that may arise in conversations between teachers and children in response to children's drawing activity. Drawing is one of the major and earliest systems which children use to represent the environment, objects, persons and events, both spontaneously and as a result of requests from teachers, other adults and children (Smith, 1983; Matthews, 1988).

In line with other arguments in this book it can be suggested that children's drawings not only represent their knowledge and experience but that drawing enables children to develop or construct further concepts (Athey, 1990). It is vital, therefore, that teachers recognize and are able to respond, not only to the characteristics of children's drawings but also to the social, cultural and contextual features that may have influenced the drawing performance, in all its aspects including the mathematical dimensions (Buckham, 1994). Teachers will benefit from understanding the different sorts of strategies and representations children are using, so that their conversations with children not only make sense to children but enable children to reflect on what they have done. We have argued elsewhere that the role of the teacher is crucial to constructivism. Teachers' interventions about children's drawings, without being interference, can occur during or after the process. Teachers can also request particular drawings in the expectation that they will include mathematical concepts for discussion.

It needs to be clear that the position taken up about art and mathematics is the same as that suggested in chapter 3 about drama and mathematics. Mathematics must not spoil or drive either art or drama. Rather we look to see what mathematical opportunities arise in drama or art and capitalize on them when they do so. This chapter uses examples of children's drawings to identify mathematical dimensions, particularly those of shape, space and time and discusses how teachers can respond.

## The Nature of Children's Drawings

The nature of young children's drawings has been discussed extensively (Golomb, 1992; Wolf and Perry, 1988). To summarize some of the more important mathematical features that appear in children's drawings, three examples drawn by four-year-old pre-school children are illustrated in Figures 8.1b, 8.1c and 8.1d. Part of the environment in which they were drawing had been set up as a forest. This environment was one which was thought might be represented in many of the children's activities, which included painting, drawing and three dimensional work.

All drawings and paintings are an arrangement of lines, shapes and colour on a flat surface. However, children have different graphic means with which to make designs or representations of objects and events according to their age and experience. Three and four-year-old children represent the attributes that they feel are necessary and important within a drawing or painting. Characteristics of a visual scene may match numbers of objects, enclosure and expressive qualities but may omit certain features of shape although children can and do use a variety of shapes in their drawings (Smith, 1992). In Figure 8.1c, Daniel has drawn an illustration at the base of his page (himself). He has used an enclosed shape to represent himself and he has used extended lines with small circular shapes at the ends to represent his legs and feet. What he has drawn is sufficient for his purposes but he has not matched the actual shapes which make up the various parts of a person. Similarly he has matched the number and position but not the shape of the butterflies found in the 'forest' set up in the classroom. Their relative positions seem more important to him than relative size or shape. The enclosed circular shape at the very top of the paper is a small toy tiger; one of a number hidden in the forest. This tiger was placed high up on a piece of furniture, covered with fabric onto which butterflies and other insects had been attached. Daniel's drawing led to a lively discussion of where he had spotted the tiger, whether he had been able to

Figure 8.1

a   Children had to crawl into the forest to find the baby tigers

b   Rachel was reminded of going into a tunnel

c   Daniel saw one of the tigers high up in the forest

d   Michelle saw tiger footprints on the ground

reach up to it and how it had been rescued. In chapter 9 the use of spatial language will be discussed and one item is the situation where children can deal with the words 'higher up'.

Figure 8.1b shows a student teacher talking to another child who had explored the forest area. This environment had enabled the children to have a wide range of visual, tactile and spatial experiences in the process of a dramatic situation, that of helping a mother tiger find cubs lost in the forest. The children had to crawl through vegetation to an enclosed play space via a narrow entrance. The student anticipated that the enclosure Rachel was painting was either the forest, or a papier mâché mountain that was in the forest or even the cave opening in the mountain where one baby tiger had been found. Much to her surprise the child announced that it was a tunnel for the train she was going to paint. Through discussion it emerged that as Rachel crawled through the forest, she said, it was just like going into the tunnel in the London Underground which she had just done.

The forest environment had a patterned cloth on the ground, strewn with leaves, feathers, pebbles and various items which could be brought back from the forest itself. The children spent much time looking down while they were moving or crawling around. Michelle's response combined painting as well as printing with three or four fingers dipped into paint. She had seen the tiger's footprints through the leaves in the forest, she said as she walked her fingers around the page describing a path which was beginning to look like a spiral (Figure 8.1d). In these three examples (8.1b, c and d) some of the important visual-spatial characteristics of the environment have been represented and in the last example, gestural movement, one of the earliest features of babies' mark making is also taking the form of an early map (Wolf *et al.*, 1988; Matthews, 1988).

These and other drawings produced after the drama session allowed the student teachers involved to make very specific links between what the children had drawn and what prompted the drawings. The range of salient features the children represented were extensive even though the graphic means they had at their disposal would appear to be limited. The mathematical understandings the children were encoding in their drawings needed to be highlighted in discussion with an adult. However, what was particularly significant in this session was the difficulty student teachers had in adjusting their expectations of what young children's drawings might show as well as what was missing.

As has been argued elsewhere (Buckham, 1994), unless teachers have a real understanding of children's drawing they will miss the significance of what it does present. Even more significantly, I would argue, teachers may miss the significance of what a drawing *might* present, given an appropriate context. Figure 8.2a is an example which highlights this argument. A six year old had made this drawing, requested by the teacher, in terms that identify the factual answer: my class teacher, my friend and my teddy (it was a giant teddy) are all taller than me and my pencil and my pencil sharpener are shorter than me. But drawing allows the possibility of considering scale and proportion visually, and the three illustrations and two objects in her drawing, although carefully constructed, bear little size relation to each other or the referent — herself. But is there any reason why they should? Mathematically the question is limited in its objective. Having satisfied that objective the child was praised for the amount of detail in the drawing especially the portrait of the class teacher (left hand illustration). Is this a valid way of finding out about children's emerging understanding of comparative measurement?

Fortunately, it is possible to look at a whole range of drawings done by this same child, both before and after Figure 8.2a, to discover some valuable features which appear to be of far greater mathematical significance than those embedded (or not) in this 'longer than, shorter than' drawing[1]. It might be noted that these sorts of drawings are very common in commercial schemes and appear to be of dubious mathematical value. Wolf and Perry (1988), amongst others, point to the fact that children between the ages of five and seven are beginning to construct drawing systems in addition to the ones they have developed, which already include rules about relative size. These new systems require the representation of objects as they are situated in a larger space.

## The Importance of Children's Drawing Systems

There is a complex interplay of forces influencing the forms of images which children use. In selecting two drawings made six months earlier than Figure 8.2a, but within days of each other, it is possible to see two very different spatial settings in Figures 8.2b and c. The arrangements are determined by the story contexts in which the drawings were done. The drawing (Figure 8.2c) of the very tiny princess on the castle battlements, 'too far away' to be caught by the king, is in fact untypical for the child, in terms of the proportion of illustrations to setting and the location of the setting within the picture frame. The new emphasis on scale and proportion has been inspired by the idea behind the drawing.

*Figure 8.2*

*a   6 years*

*b   5 years   'The Princess is going to marry the bear and the Prince is saying I hate that bear'*

*c   5 years   'The King wanted to catch the Princess but she is too far away'*

*d   6 years   'Tom wanted to catch Jerry'*

On the other hand, the characters in Figure 8.2b bear no particular spatial relation to the castle, except of being inside it. The focus of this drawing is similar to that of Figure 8.2a in its detail. It has clearly differentiated crowns and clothing but most important is the meaning of the facial expressions of the prince and princess. The bear's face has no particular expression, but the slight space between him and the princess and the overlapping of the princess and the prince could appear to suggest an expressive tension; the bear almost appears to be dragging the princess away from the hapless prince. These two drawings underline one of the important characteristics of drawing itself and that is the way it combines objective and expressive modes of thinking.

Objective and expressive modes of thinking need to be appreciated when evaluating children's drawings and the extent to which they may indicate some awareness of, for example, comparative measurement or proportion. The drawing of Tom and Jerry, Figure 8.2d, was carried out three months earlier than Figure 8.2a. This drawing is also untypical, amongst many drawings done at that time, yet it appeared in a classroom situation no different from any other that term. It appears to indicate an out of classroom experience which, for whatever reason, had been vividly recalled. The framing of the Tom and Jerry scene, by the edges of the page and the consequent cropping of the lady just above the waist are sophisticated procedures that suggest that they have been inspired by conventions common to film, television and comics (Wilson, Hurwitz and Wilson, 1987).

The depiction of Tom's owner calls for an indication of comparative size but the particular event being imagined has prompted an awareness of distance and position which can be described both spatially and expressively. Figure 8.2d is also an example of the way drawing can depict a particular moment in time but also suggests movement and duration of time. In cinematic terms the single frame or still image is never seen in isolation and the construction of this drawing presupposes the time before and the action which is taking place and is continuing into the future. Within the image itself, movement is suggested by the multiple lines of the arms of the lady holding Tom and other observable features of the drawn image. This sense of movement is an illusory one (Werner and Kaplan, 1963) but compelling none the less.

Having looked at drawings done before the mathematics lesson, Figure 8.2a, it is instructive to look at one done at home at the same time (Figure 8.3). This drawing shows a section of a house with its sole occupant (a man) in the sitting room downstairs. In this large-scale

Figure 8.3

*6 years 'A man in his house'*

complex drawing the child has set herself the task of not just describing the various items of furniture in each room, but the relative size of each. She has even differentiated between the light fittings in each room which range from a medium-sized ceiling fitting in the kitchen to large paper lanterns in two upstairs rooms and a giant chandelier in the sitting room. This drawing also shows a range of strategies which she had devised for showing that objects are three dimensional. Children's drawings are frequently criticized as being poor representations of the three dimensional world because:

It is commonly thought that a representation is an attempt to reproduce the image that enters the eye, but this is a misunderstanding. It would be closer to the truth to say that graphic representation is a process of selecting from our visual and non-visual knowledge, features of objects and making a match between these and visual-graphic properties of the materials we are working with (Smith, 1983).

I have described the house as a section rather than a view or X-ray picture, as such drawings are sometimes mistakenly called. As the statement above suggests, making a match between visual and non-visual knowledge and the graphic properties and means available, allows for the generation of a variety of possible drawing systems. Also, there is no reason why several systems should not be employed in the same drawing. At the stage where children are still combining topological[1] and emerging projective systems, to speak of a view, implying a single (X-ray) viewpoint, is not really appropriate. Throughout this chapter, examples of topological and projective geometry are in evidence and there are very few instances of children employing aspects of the system known as 'perspective'. The term perspective is used very widely in a general sense to describe any drawing that attempts to show depth or to be realistic in any way. Perspective has been usefully separated from this general meaning by (Dubery and Willats, 1983) and others' use of the notion of topological and projective drawing systems to describe the rules that quite separate systems employ. Lack of familiarity with the rules that do govern identifiable drawing systems that children generate and how successfully children use them, has frequently led to undervaluation of children's mathematical thinking. A further aspect that is of particular importance in any discussion of the way children employ drawing systems as they get older is that of the development of a drawing repertoire. There has been, traditionally, a somewhat narrow view of drawing development (Wolf and Perry, 1988).

The drawing of a man in his house, Figure 8.3, has been seen by many adults and without careful looking and sometimes only after prompting, it appears that many have difficulty in recognizing the cooker in the left handside, lower part of the drawing. It is frequently mistaken for a stacking stereo and apart from contextual reasons, this is usually because of the way it is drawn. However, the system used to represent the cooker is an identifiable one and its rules require the front and top faces of objects to be shown one above the other in a vertical arrangement. Dubery and Willats (1983) describe this system as 'vertical oblique projection' and suggest that rather than showing a net (although this drawn cooker has striking similarities to this concept) this is in fact a form of projection assuming a high viewpoint some distance away (see also Willats, 1985 and 1992).

Drawing systems which are closer to the concept of a net are often termed 'fold out' and the resulting drawn objects or scenes need to be looked at carefully to identify the various orientations involved. This topological process is often seen alongside vertical projection and there are several examples of both in a drawing made by the same child, Figure 8.9 when she was five (Buckham, 1994).

There are a number of items in the house, Figure 8.3, which are constructed in a similar way to the cooker, including the sofa, a small table and a large chair in the sitting room. In other places objects are drawn as if viewed from the side and in the bathroom (top right) a toothbrush holder and a washbasin are lined up against the drawn edge on the right, suggesting a side wall boundary. Yet another system is used to show the space relations between the man and the large chair. The term occlusion is used to describe the way one object comes in front of another and partially or wholly obscures it. This child had in fact used this device intermittently from a very early age, although the system generally occurs infrequently in very young children's drawing (Athey, 1991).

On the small table beside the man there is a framed photograph. Although she wanted to show that it was on the table she has shown it separately, as a small rectangle, above the larger rectangle that denotes the table top. Rather than draw it enclosed within the table top, or with even more difficulty, half in the table top and half above, she has chosen to draw it separately. In doing this she gives less ambiguous information about space relations and this is quite consistent with findings reported by Willats (1992), Cox (1991) and others. This principle is also in operation in the drawing of the vases of flowers both on the kitchen table and on the table in the bedroom (upper left hand part of the drawing) The drawn lines of the surface areas of the two tables have been obscured by heavy oil pastel colouring and so the device is less obvious.

One part of the picture which excites comment from many adults is the way that the bed appears to be shown by a method something akin to the rules of perspective. There is a suggestion, in the drawing, that the vertical lines enclosed by the curved ends of the bed are joined at the base at various points along two imaginary converging diagonal lines. This illusion is heightened by the sloping lines of the adjacent bookcase. This may be more of an accident than deliberate construction but it is often through chance occurrences that new learning can take place. Certainly discussion of such features may have a significant impact on older children or children who are at a point when they are ready to consolidate previous tentative experiments in the same area. In this child's case, it is possible to see such tentative moves (as in Figure 8.4a). It was not until her final year in primary school that she, like many other children of that age, occasionally attempted to use converging rather than parallel lines.

## Work from Observation, Memory, Imagination and Work about Time

The selection, arrangement and descriptions of items in Figure 8.4a can be seen in relation to the actual objects the child was drawing: Figure 8.4b. Even when children work from close observation, and this was an extremely rare event in this particular child's experience, they are not replicating the scene in front of them like cameras, but so often they are judged as if they were. Drawing from a fixed point is an extremely narrow task as it admits no deviation or movement. Much frustration could be avoided if drawing from observation was seen as matching objectively the most appropriate features of an object or scene whilst at the same time matching aesthetically the very essence of what is being depicted: its sensory and expressive characteristics (Smith, 1992). The drawing of the objects in Figure 8.4a is a good example of how young children's graphic means naturally suggest movement and a comparison with the rather static character of the group of objects she chose to draw. Figure 8.4b (a reconstruction of the items selected from what was a very crowded corner of a room) shows this clearly.

The fact that this six year old chose to draw this group of objects in the first place can be explained in various ways. One of them, undoubtedly, was linked to the fact that she had visited an art exhibition a few hours earlier and had been captivated by the experience. During the course of the afternoon, she had drawn from memory, a female illustration she had admired as a sculpture in the exhibition. She had also drawn from memory a building in Central London. Prior to this observational drawing (Figure 8.4a) she had drawn an imaginary scene of Adam and Eve, with two animals in the Garden of Eden. This momentum in drawing activity culminated in her choosing a rather challenging and unfamiliar task. I would suggest that the examples of artists' work, she had seen, had provided a powerful range of models for her to emulate in her own production. I would also link her choice of

Figure 8.4

a   6 years                    b

I like baking because we do it at home.

c   5 years

objects to an interest she often showed in her work: that of shape and space. By comparing the drawing (Figure 8.4a) with the photograph of the reconstruction (Figure 8.4b) the shape and space aspects of the scene she has represented become quite clear.

She has described the relation between the horizontal mat on the desk and the vertical and horizontal lines of the angle-poise lamp. She has also located the framed print and shown its top edge as a diagonal line. She has shown how an ornamental bird has been partially occluded by this frame. Only the bird's head and beak protrude and a leg pokes down onto the mat below. The bird and small toy illustration hanging from the lamp in the drawing are longer in scale than the real objects. This may be because these objects were of special interest to her. However, children, like adult artists, are not only responding to the items they are observing but also to the marks they are making on the paper. The drawing must be satisfactory, to the drawer, in itself as well as in the way it represents its referent. The sort of experience this child had already had as a perceiver of art earlier in the afternoon is similar to the experience of looking at her own work and making decisions about this (Wolf, 1989). The extent, in particular, to which children have internalized certain mathematical understandings plays a crucial role at this stage.

The fact that both this drawing (Figure 8.4a) and the one discussed previously, (Figure 8.3) were made by the same child outside school, and the extent to which they show more mathematically significant understanding than any drawing task completed at school in that year suggests two things. Firstly, as Art in the National Curriculum (DES, 1992) has suggested in the non-statutory guidance, evidence of children's work out of school could provide a useful contribution towards any assessment of children's achievements. Given the nature of children's drawings, these contributions could apply to a range of subjects in the curriculum, including mathematics. Secondly the substantial evidence that children often create art work out of school in a way which is qualitatively different from much 'school art' (Taylor, 1986; Wilson, 1992) requires that attention is paid to the factors that contribute to these differences. A major factor is the role that the work of adult artists plays in children's work. Wolf (1989) describes the sort of learning which takes place through the interaction of the various acts of making and perceiving art as 'conversation' and it is the sort of conversation which has already been referred to in the discussion on Figure 8.4a. The role of the teacher in such 'conversations' as suggested earlier, is an important one. The drawing of Tom and Jerry (Figure 8.2d) whilst illustrating a piece of writing, also provides the sort of opportunity for discussion that can highlight culturally significant phenomena in art and mathematics. This is in much the same way that teachers might use Egyptian wall painting to discuss the culturally derived mathematical rules that governed their artistic design.

As Wilson and Ligtvoet (1992), Court (1992) and Varkalis (1992) have shown in such diverse countries as modern Egypt, Japan, Holland, Italy, Kenya and the United Kingdom, culturally specific factors play a very significant role in understanding children's art and the mathematical implications of their findings are equally important, not least for teachers. Introducing children to the work of artists from a variety of cultures may also be a way of confirming, both to children and their teachers, that many of the drawing systems children construct are of value in themselves. They are not simply steps on the way to a single 'end point' of drawing development, to be forgotten or devalued at a later date (Matthews, 1991).

Children do continue to use a whole range of systems unless they are dissuaded from doing so. Unfortunately, this is very often the case and some of the factors which may be contributory are adult views of those aspects of art and mathematics discussed so far.

In order to broaden concepts of shape and space in drawings a consideration of both of these and how they include time is relevant. Figure 8.4c is a drawing that deserves careful consideration, in this respect, as it is a wonderful example of the ease with which young children may create their own meanings, through drawing, both in response to a teacher's task and by moving beyond it.

Lee and his year-one class had been making bread with their student teacher. She asked them to record in visual form the sequence in which they had carried out the activities. The drawings were to form part of a class book so with each child's contribution she was able to cover virtually every aspect of the experience the children had. By getting the children to divide their page into four she intended them to show a time sequence, but as a result of giving the children a plain sheet of paper, some children drew a grid rather than folding their paper into four and Lee allowed space for writing below his grid. At first sight this drawing might appear like Figure 8.3, showing four separate rooms in a house, but closer inspection reveals the same arrangement repeated in boxes 1, 2, 3 and then the introduction of the oven, with diagonal wavy lines indicating heat and the absence of illustrations makes box 4 quite different. What sequence in the baking process is intended by steps 1–3 is difficult to read from the drawing. However, what this drawing goes on to show constitutes a difficult concept for children to grasp fully and that is the notion of time as continuous. Lee

shows an illustration outside the framework of the required task, carry-
ing out an activity related to the timescale of box 4: a child is washing
his hands while the bread is baking. The positioning of this illustration
at the end of a pathway leading from the baking scene into a space
where a notional fifth sequence would have been drawn is an interesting one and may indicate the spatial dimension that an initial glimpse
of the drawing suggested (some of the children left the classroom to
wash their hands in the cloakroom after the session and this may be
reflected in this detail). Amongst other things the element of simultane-
ous events in time could have been discussed with Lee.

The drawings of birds in the classroom from close observation
(Figures 8.5a and b) highlight dimensions of time and space and their
interdependence rather poignantly. Sometimes it is possible to miss
some of the more subtle qualities in children's drawings without careful
consideration. In Figure 8.5a the strong overall geometric design and
the grid-like structure of the bird's cage is immediately striking. By
contrast the drawing of the same subject by another child (Figure 8.5b)
may be considered less bold in structure and arrangement and less
immediate but more subtle in its visual impact. The structure of the
cage appears a little lopsided and the white window frame is rather
thick in relation to the size of the individual panes, but the detail is
rather intriguing. If one considers the two drawings in terms of how
much space they suggest or how much movement is conjured up even
more differences are evident. The space around the cage in Figure 8.5a,
is divided into three sections and coloured in, creating a more abstract
surround than in Figure 8.5b where the classroom space is suggested
much more specifically. The broken lines of the horizontal bars of the
cage in Figure 8.5b, as well as the vigorous marks of the chalks and
charcoal, all suggest a sense of movement. Further areas like the strong
arc diagonally over the cage heighten this impression. This arc is also
a strong linking device which draws attention to the content of the
scene. Wild birds hover in flight at the classroom window looking in,
whilst the budgies sit in their cage. This imaginative situation heightens
awareness of spatial and temporal dimensions in a way that could be
deepened through discussion and can be beneficial from both a mathematical and art perspective. Spending some time looking at this drawing and then returning to look at Figure 8.5a may result in a different
perception of the previous scene; the scale of the birds may suggest
they are cramped and constrained by their cage space. This underlines
the delicate balance any form of assessment of drawing requires between observable, quantifiable facts and more expressive features. One
way of exploring these is in discussion when further dimensions of the

Figure 8.5

a   7/8 years

b   7/8 years

child's intentions, other perceptions and links with similar features in the work of other artists may be appropriate.

Recording from observation aspects of the school environment is frequently carried out to develop children's drawing skills and a particularly rewarding area may be the school hall with PE equipment as a focus of interest. Figure 8.6 is a drawing based on observation of the hall during a PE lesson but this is not solely a drawing from observation. It is an illustration of a poem that each child in the class had written about an aspect of PE and in this child's case, she had written about an unruly class, a teacher not quite in control, the momentary calm that had resulted from the head's appearance and then the return to chaos. As a unit of time a PE lesson is clearly defined and it is interesting that the child has included part of the clock on the wall, cut off by the left hand edge of the paper. The pupils are placed at various points in the drawing like counters on a snakes and ladders board and throughout there is a tension between moving and still illustrations, stable and precarious poses and vertical, horizontal and diagonal lines.

The passage of time is described by two visual conventions. The first is a long curly line linking the boy on the low bench (left hand side with one leg stretched out behind) and the teacher who is standing on the floor just off centre with a long 'Help' balloon coming out of her mouth. She has been hit by a ball or bean bag that Daniel has just thrown and the curly line describes its flight path. This comic and cartoon device along with the speech bubbles, names and arrows is not a particularly strong visual feature but the second device is and at the same time has links with cinematic devices mentioned earlier in connection with the Tom and Jerry drawing. The second convention consists of placing similar items in slightly different positions to suggest movement. The way the ropes have been drawn suggests three stages of their momentum, diminishing in swing from left to right. This device can be effective in exploring more complex sequences of movement in space as numerous artists have explored, particularly since the advent of photography and cinematography.

## Conclusion

The previous drawings — Figures 8.4c, 8.5a, 8.5b and 8.6 — have opened up discussion of some of the different functions that drawing can have and within those drawings sensory characteristics such as motion and duration have been considered. As children get older they gain an increasing 'repertoire' of drawing systems amongst which to

*8 years*

choose. The rules which govern each system also relate to when they might be appropriate. A drawing that uses the edge of the drawing paper like a co-ordinate frame (Figure 8.6) differs in other important respects from Figure 8.7a or Figure 8.7b but all three depend on the increasing depth of knowledge about measurement and scale that children acquire as they go through school. Figure 8.7a, although carried out a little earlier than Figure 8.6 is by the same child. Here, she is concerned to convey a specific scale-related image of her drawing of a girl in a city scene. In the PE picture, it is less important to her that the children should be consistently in scale with each other, the teacher and the surroundings, than that they should be carefully spaced and located at many levels in the drawing.

The girl is in Figure 8.7a is most certainly in scale with her environment. As her confidence and stance suggest, she is very much at home in the city. It is no coincidence that the child who did the drawing had been with her school to the National Gallery in London and had been inspired by the discussion with teachers in the gallery in front of a range of paintings including portraits. They considered the relationships of individuals to their settings, including some on a magnificent scale. The visual images that scale and projection might add to the status of the people in the portraits is reflected in Figure 8.7a and other drawings the child did at the same time, mainly outside school.

There are three further drawings by this child made at around the age of 11 — Figures 8.7b, 8.8a, 8.8b and another — Figure 8.10 — by a boy the same age. Between them they show a range of understanding and handling of scale, space and time that illustrate some of the many different ways in which children may be working, at this stage from their own repertoire. The boy who drew the imaginary traffic drama — Figure 8.10 discovered a completely new dimension in drawing after he and other children in his class had been studying aerial photographs. He combined scale, space and time to produce a particularly satisfying and aesthetically pleasing outcome. Although quite different in spatial arrangement, Figures 8.8a and 8.8b indicate further explorations in scale and proportion. Figure 8.8b shows the elongated and slender illustration of one of the main characters in a story book made at school. Her proportions have been inspired by studying fashion drawings at home and applying their conventions to a different context. That children should be confident enough to do this is important as well as being an enriching experience.

Finally, Figures 8.9 and 8.10 give readers the opportunity to look closely and identify for themselves features which have been discussed throughout this chapter. There is a difference of six years between

Figures 8.7

b   11 years   Design for front cover of school short-story project

a   8 years

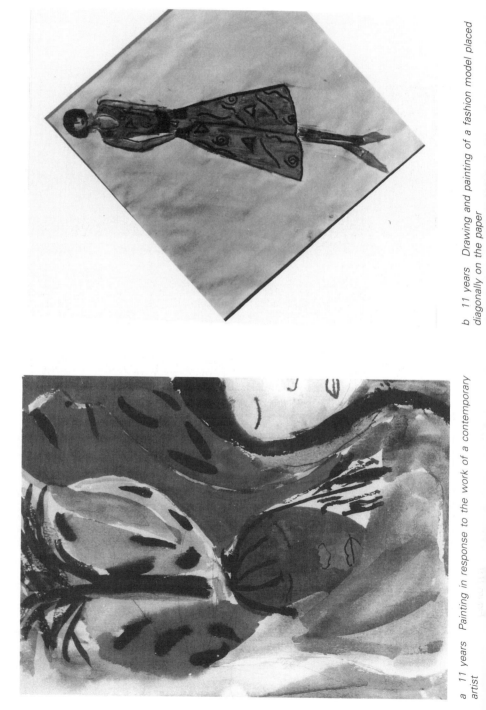

*Figure 8.8*

134

*b 11 years Drawing and painting of a fashion model placed diagonally on the paper*

*a 11 years Painting in response to the work of a contemporary artist*

Figure 8.9

5 years   Drawing of journey to Devon and a summer holiday with friends

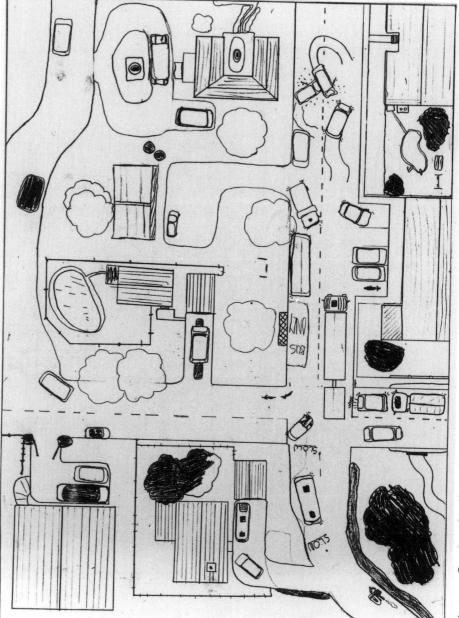

*Figure 8.10*

11 years  Drawing of traffic accident

these two children which illustrates that as development occurs, drawing repertoire expands, many features are retained and refined, and new ones are introduced while others are left behind. I have argued that, as suggested in the introduction, it is possible to deepen our understanding of both mathematics and art through the study of children's drawings and children drawing.

## Note

Topology is important to mathematics and geography as well as art. It can be defined, mathematically, as a branch of geometry concerned with properties of shape which remain the same even when the shape itself is deformed. Thus a circle and a square are topologically equivalent. A three-dimensional example might be that a piece of plasticene could be moulded into either a cup or a doughnut shape. The two would be topologically equivalent if the hole — in the cup handle or the middle of the doughnut — were retained. Topology, therefore is not concerned with measurement. It is about a class of relationships such as how one shape is found within another, closed and open shapes and the relationships between spaces such as their insides and outsides or how they are distributed. Primary children can use and understand certain aspects of topology and need to do so because, although it is hard to define it is an essential element in understanding space and shape.

# 9 Mathematics Beyond the School and a Summing Up

*Deirdre Pettitt and Andrew Davis*

## Introduction

In chapter 2 we discussed the nature of mathematics, arguing, amongst other things, that the subject should not be divorced from 'human activities, interactions and rules'. The puzzling combination of human invention and objectivity which we noted exists in mathematics may have had the effect of causing it to be seen as the exclusive property of mathematicians. These mathematicians, we suggested, could be seen as delving deeper and deeper into abstractions, separating them from a 'majority of lesser mortals'. Indeed, it is possible that a view such as this has contributed to excusing a large number of otherwise educated people from feeling inadequate, instead of being quite proud when they announce that mathematics is a closed book to them. It does not surprise us when such statements are made. We can also feel it to be an unfortunate fact of life that from quite an early age mathematics for many people is boring, incomprehensible, useless, alarming or all of these. Mathematics teaching is improving. We know too many skilled and devoted teachers at all levels to doubt this. These teachers are, however, still faced with an attitude to mathematics which does not help them. Perhaps we need to be and ought to be surprised that educated people claim to be totally ignorant about mathematics. We should be surprised if they boasted of illiteracy. Perhaps the inevitability that many people find mathematics boring, irrelevant and the like needs to be challenged. Human minds presumably do not permit more than a very few people to be polymaths. However, it is a great pity that rather more people than necessary seem to be entirely cut off from one substantial and fascinating body of human experience. At least for practical purposes and to a reasonable level of understanding we might aspire to the attitude that to be educated involves feeling fairly comfortable about mathematics.

Most of the authors of this book have had many years of experience of teaching how to teach mathematics to primary education students. All of these students, currently, have GCSE mathematics or an equivalent at Grade C or better. Even amongst these able young people we find some who claim that their success stems from rote learning and they are nervous about teaching children. Similarly, skilled administrative staff of our acquaintance, dealing with complex accounts, have told us that they wanted to go further than they did in mathematics. These people, and the students, often give the same explanation for giving up on mathematics. This is, that at a certain point in their schooling, they no longer understood the mathematics (which they were often able to do successfully) nor did they understand what it was for or what connection it had with everyday experience. We can surmise that these able people had lost the 'mental map' of relational understanding to which we referred in chapter 2. It seems clear that well before the point at which these people lost their way, and at various points in their school careers many children also become baffled. Given the notorious '7 year Gap' (Cockroft, 1984) found between some children entering secondary school, losing your way occurs in the primary as well as the secondary school. We are not concerned here with children who fail in the secondary school where teachers are generally well qualified to teach mathematics. However, a possible explanation for some children's discomfort with mathematics in the secondary school might be considered by both secondary and primary teachers. It is that when you are good at mathematics it can become difficult to 'decenter' (Donaldson, 1978) and to realize that what is obvious to you can be very obscure to your pupils.

On the other hand it is the case that primary teachers need a solid relational understanding of mathematics to a considerably higher level than the ceilings of most primary school children. It is hardly possible to help children to acquire 'networks of connections' (Haylock and Cockburn, 1989), to see patterns and solve problems, all of which are being argued for in this book, if mathematics puzzles the teacher. The sorts of discussions we have recommended can tax teachers' knowledge. Teachers may 'shut down' if temporarily thrown by a child's question. However, teachers have the power and the ability to find out answers and as McNamara (1994) points out, teachers often learn more about mathematics by teaching it.

In chapter 4 Brian Woodhouse demonstrated how investigations at an adult level can involve teachers in a clearer understanding of constraints and variables. These, at ascending levels of difficulty, enable teachers to develop and improve logical and methodological strategies which, in due course lead to the identification of proofs in the secondary school (and sometimes earlier). In investigations, problem solving and discussion about mathematics teachers as well as children may see patterns and connections which either they had not been aware of or which, in the case of teachers, had been forgotten or obscured over time. So, we suggest that the sorts of mathematical experiences we have recommended are within the grasp of teachers who, where necessary, can re-construct their own subject knowledge.

We are recommending some changes to mathematics teaching — mainly alongside and augmenting existing practice — in the primary school to practitioners who are already overburdened. Unlike others who exhort teachers to do better (and in the certain knowledge that improving their teaching is the aim of primary teachers) we have offered some practical advice. This may be timely, in view of the focus on core subjects and the extra time available to teachers on the implementation of the Dearing Report (Dearing, 1994). However, we also need to make a case for what we have suggested being worth the effort. It would not be, if only a few children could benefit and those would rise to the top however they were taught. There is a good deal of evidence, however, that children have the propensity to be good at mathematics and we turn to some of this evidence in the next section.

## Learning Before Schooling

There will always be a wide variation in experience and attainment of school children and the Reception class is no exception. Having conceded this point we can examine some of the evidence about the mathematics that children bring to school. Much of this relates to number.

Extensive research now supports the view that children have a strong rule-governed grasp of aspects of mathematics. Gelman and Gallistell (1978) showed how children impose patterns on their experience of counting. More recently Carpenter *et al.* (1982) has shown that pre-schoolers can successfully work out word problems in addition and subtraction providing the quantities are small. My study (Desforges ànd Desforges, 1980) demonstrated that four year olds had developed a number-based notion of 'fair' sharing of sweets and had a variety of strategies for dealing with remainders. More recently Martin Hughes (1986) has confirmed that youngsters can develop and use symbol systems to represent small quantities (Desforges, 1989).

Commenting on these and other achievements of pre-schoolers, Desforges (*ibid.*) suggests that 'sufficient is known . . . for teachers to be optimistic about what can be achieved . . .' Over the past few years and ongoing, research at the University of Durham — hereinafter called the Durham Project — has amongst other things, tested the mathematics which children bring to school (Aubrey, 1994 and forthcoming). The results of testing over 150 children's ability in number in the first few weeks in school or in nursery schools have been consistent with the findings mentioned above. To illustrate this we show in Tables 9.1 and 9.2 some of the results of testing basic knowledge about number, particularly counting, of 50 children in two different nursery schools. The tests were administered towards the end of the summer term to children who would enter Reception classes in the following September. The mean age of the children was approximately 4 years 6 months. (An approximate figure is given because the testing spanned about two months as each complete test took about 3 hours.) The two nurseries were very different: 'Arlington' was attached to a primary school in an ex-mining village near Durham and most children entered that school; 'Beever Lane' was in a Durham town, not attached to a school and had a wide variety of pupils who would disperse to many different schools in September.

As the headings are brief a fuller explanation is needed. 'Recite' is the highest number children would count to, over two trials, without omission, repetition or error. This gives a conservative figure as many children went much further on one trial and almost all of them said many more numbers, usually in the right order but with omissions. For example, many were aware of the decade system and would follow, say, 20 by 30, 40, 50, etc. You will notice that given objects to count some children could go beyond the number they were willing to recite. Alternatively, some could recite to quite a high number but could not apply the skill to a practical task. Overall, however, the majority of children could use the numbers they could recite, at least within 10. That is they had one:one correspondence, some principles of cardinality and some of order irrelevance (it doesn't matter in what order you count a collection of objects, the cardinal number is the same).

These items (one:one correspondence, cardinality and order irrelevance) are shown in columns 2 — 11. Children were asked to count 3 objects in a line, 3 in a pile, 7 in a line, 7 in a circle, to give the researcher 4 from 12 and 10 from 12 (columns 2 — 7). Columns

Table 9.1: Arlington Nursery School

| | Recite | 3 in line | 3 in pile | 7 in line | 7 in circle | 4 from 12 | 10 from 12 | 4 R→L | 6 R→L | 4 from 2nd | 6 from 2nd | Recognize |
|---|---|---|---|---|---|---|---|---|---|---|---|---|
| 1 | 13 | yes | yes | yes | yes | yes | yes | yes | yes | yes | yes | 1–8 |
| 2 | 13 | yes | yes | yes | yes | yes | yes | yes | yes | yes | yes | 1–9 |
| 3 | 10 | yes | yes | yes | yes | yes | yes | yes | yes | no | no | 1, 3, 4, 5, 6 |
| 4 | 11 | yes | yes | no | no | no | no | yes | no | no | no | nil |
| 5 | 7 | yes | yes | no | no | no | no | yes | no | no | no | nil |
| 6 | 9 | yes | yes | yes | yes | yes | yes | yes | yes | yes | yes | 1, 3 |
| 7 | 11 | yes | yes | yes | yes | yes | no | yes | yes | yes | yes | 1–10 |
| 8 | 12 | yes | yes | yes | yes | yes | yes | yes | no | yes | yes | nil |
| 9 | 9 | yes | yes | yes | yes | yes | no | no | yes | no | no | 1–10 |
| 10 | 29 | yes | yes | yes | yes | yes | yes | yes | yes | yes | yes | 1–10 |
| 11 | 26 | yes | yes | yes | yes | yes | yes | yes | yes | yes | yes | 1–7 |
| 12 | 11 | yes | yes | yes | yes | yes | no | no | no | no | no | nil |
| 13 | 2 | yes | yes | yes | yes | yes | no | no | no | yes | no | 3, 4 |
| 14 | 20 | yes | yes | yes | yes | yes | yes | yes | yes | yes | yes | 1, 3, 4, 5, 6, 7, 8, 9 |
| 15 | 12 | yes | yes | no | no | yes | yes | yes | no | no | no | nil |
| 16 | 11 | yes | yes | yes | yes | yes | | yes | yes | yes | yes | 1, 2, 3, 4, 5, 6, 7, 8, 10 |
| 17 | 9 | no | yes | no | no | no | no | yes | no | no | no | 1–10 |
| 18 | 11 | yes | yes | yes | yes | yes | no | yes | no | yes | no | nil |
| 19 | 13 | yes | yes | no | no | yes | no | no | yes | no | no | 1, 2, 3, 4, 5, 6, 7, 9 |
| 20 | 50 | yes | yes | yes | yes | yes | yes | yes | yes | yes | yes | 1–10 |
| 21 | 9 | yes | yes | no | no | yes | no | no | no | yes | no | nil |
| 22 | 11 | yes | no | yes | yes | yes | yes | yes | yes | yes | no | 1, 3, 4, 9 |
| 23 | 4 | yes | yes | no | no | no | no | yes | no | yes | no | nil |
| 24 | 14 | yes | yes | yes | yes | no | yes | yes | yes | no | no | 1, 3, 4, 5, 6, 7, 8, 9 |

Table 9.2: *Beever Lane Nursery School*

| | Recite | 3 in line | 3 in pile | 7 in line | 7 in circle | 4 from 12 | 10 from 12 | 4 R→L | 6 R→L | 4 from 2nd | 6 from 2nd | Recognize |
|---|---|---|---|---|---|---|---|---|---|---|---|---|
| 25 | 20 | yes | yes | yes | yes | yes | yes | yes | yes | yes | yes | 1–10 |
| 26 | 28 | yes | yes | yes | yes | yes | yes | yes | yes | yes | yes | 1–10 |
| 27 | 10 | yes | yes | yes | yes | yes | yes | yes | yes | no | no | 1, 3, 4, 5, 6, 7, 8, |
| 28 | 30 | yes | yes | yes | yes | yes | yes | yes | yes | no | no | 1–10 |
| 29 | 20 | yes | yes | yes | yes | yes | no | yes | yes | yes | yes | 1, 2, 3, 4, 5, 6, 7, 9, 10 |
| 30 | 19 | yes | yes | yes | yes | no | no | yes | yes | no | no | 1, 4 |
| 31 | 29 | yes | yes | yes | no | yes | yes | yes | yes | no | no | 1–8 |
| 32 | 28 | yes | yes | yes | no | yes | yes | yes | yes | yes | yes | 1, 2, 3, 4 |
| 33 | 5 | yes | yes | no | no | yes | no | yes | yes | no | no | 1, 3, 4, 6 |
| 34 | 15 | yes | yes | yes | yes | no | no | yes | yes | no | no | nil |
| 35 | 13 | yes | yes | yes | yes | yes | yes | yes | yes | yes | yes | 1, 2, 3, 4 |
| 36 | 19 | yes | yes | yes | yes | yes | yes | yes | yes | no | yes | 1–10 |
| 37 | 34 | yes | yes | yes | yes | yes | yes | yes | yes | no | no | 1–10 |
| 38 | 12 | yes | yes | yes | yes | yes | yes | yes | yes | no | no | 1–10 |
| 39 | 8 | no | no | no | no | yes | no | yes | yes | no | no | nil |
| 40 | 29 | yes | yes | yes | yes | yes | yes | yes | yes | yes | yes | 1, 2, 3, 4, 5, 6, 7, 9, 10 |
| 41 | 20 | yes | yes | yes | yes | yes | yes | yes | yes | no | no | 1–10 |
| 42 | 14 | yes | yes | yes | yes | yes | yes | yes | yes | yes | yes | 1, 2, 3, 4, 6 |
| 43 | 15 | yes | yes | no | yes | yes | yes | yes | yes | yes | yes | 1–10 |
| 44 | 10 | yes | yes | yes | no | yes | no | yes | yes | no | no | nil |
| 45 | 5 | yes | yes | yes | no | no | no | yes | no | no | no | 1, 2 |
| 46 | 69 | yes | yes | yes | yes | yes | yes | yes | yes | yes | yes | 1–10 |
| 47 | 100 | yes | yes | yes | yes | yes | yes | yes | yes | yes | yes | 1–10 |
| 48 | 79 | yes | yes | yes | yes | yes | no | yes | yes | yes | no | 1–10 |
| 49 | 10 | yes | yes | yes | yes | yes | yes | yes | yes | yes | yes | 1–10 |
| 50 | 15 | yes | yes | yes | yes | yes | yes | yes | yes | no | no | 1–10 |

8 — 11 show what happened when children were asked to count 4 and then 6 objects from right to left and then 4 and 6 objects making the second object the first one they counted. Column 12 shows the written numerals from 1 — 10 that each child could name.

Only a small part of the data is included here, but this illustrates the wide differences in attainment teachers in Reception classes can expect. The data provided also suggest that many children do know a lot about mathematics when they enter Reception classes and this is not the whole story. We have not included our evidence that when children have the basic counting skills shown in the tables they can use them to do a lot more. For example, if they could count with understanding to 10 they could invariably tell us or show us that you need 5 more pence to make 3 pence up to 8 pence and conversely could deduct 4 pence to reduce 7 pence to leave 3 pence. These tests involved giving a panda the right money to buy an ice cream. They could also share 4 sweets between two bears and 9 sweets between 3 bears. They were not thrown by sharing 5 sweets fairly between two bears, mainly telling us to put the one over back in the box, although two ate the one over, six gave it to another toy, two asked for another sweet and two gave the more sophisticated answer that the sweet should be halved. These last two were high counters (child No. 32 and child No. 47) but it is worth noting that one of the two who asked for another sweet, which is also enterprising, was child No. 13 who could only count to two. Given the opportunity and the situation children can surprise us by their invention. The Durham Project (*ibid.*), together with evidence from many sources, some of which were indicated above, illustrate that children, given the opportunity, are inventive and attempt, often successfully, to impose meaning on their experience. Desforges (1986) discussing children's 'inventive capacities' demonstrated in studies conducted by Piaget's followers, for example Perret-Claremont (1980), suggests that: 'social exchanges were perceived to have provoked conflicting thought. New ideas were enacted in response·to these intellectual demands' (Desforges, 1989).

We shall return to the relationship between 'intellectual demands' in a research project and classroom activities at the end of this summary. Before that, we can examine certain other mathematical achievements demonstrated in the study.

The Durham Project used Level 1 of Mathematics 5–16 (1992) (which has subsequently been revised) as a ceiling for testing. This meant that as well as number, other attainment targets were addressed. Full details are forthcoming. However, taking the same group of 50 nursery children whose achievements in number were shown above, it may be of interest to show what these children made of tests for the language of measurement, spatial language (in, under, etc.) and sorting (data handling).

## The Language of Measurement

Table 9.3 is rather negative in that it shows the error pattern, i.e. the language of measurement that children did not, on this occasion at least, know. There were 23 items in all, which were implemented by children being asked to look at and, where appropriate, handle the material provided. None of it was pictures. Unsurprisingly, there was not all that much consistency of error. One child who made six errors failed to respond correctly at items 3, 5, 6, 7, 9 and 12 and one made three errors at items 10, 11 and 23. Children only had one chance to respond although questions were clarified if it seemed necessary.

The positive aspect is the children's success. Six children knew all 23 words, fourteen children knew 22 words, six knew 21, three knew 20, five knew 19, four knew 18, three knew 17, three knew 16, three knew 15, two knew 14 and the lowest score — 13 — was achieved by two children.

Of interest to teachers may be those words which seem to cause most problems and of course those which do not. Some of the latter are hardly surprising, but it is interesting how few children were troubled by 'highest'. They can be confused between higher and taller (do I become taller or higher than you if I stand on a chair?) and later we shall see that it is a difficult spatial word. Presumably children found it easy during the test because we had (with great difficulty) constructed kites from coloured paper, which 'flew' at the end of thin sticks and one could be demonstrably seen to be higher or lower or lowest when two or three were 'flown' together and kite flying is often within children's experience.

Experience and ordinary speech may explain why 'shortest pencil' and 'shortest teddy' caused many problems. As Haylock and Cockburn (1989) point out it is more common to use the positive or dominant form of measurement language; for example taller not shorter, new not old, more not less. They suggest that both need to be presented at once, i.e. if that is heavier that must be lighter. Another possible explanation for difficulties with 'shorter' is that normal speech rarely refers to shortness except in respect of people. We refer to tall buildings but not, normally, to short buildings. As I have suggested elsewhere (Palmer and Pettitt, 1993) it may be preferable to follow normal speech for this

Table 9.3:  *Beever Lane Nursery and Arlington Nursery (Error count when children were asked, e.g. 'Show me which doll is smaller given two dolls'.)*

| Test No. | Size | |
|---|---|---|
| 1 | smaller doll of 2 | 4 |
| 2 | biggest doll of 3 | 0 |
| 3 | smallest doll of 3 | 3 |
| 4 | longer pencil of 2 | 0 |
| 5 | shortest pencil of 3 | 17 |
| 6 | longest pencil of 3 | 4 |
| 7 | thinner pencil of 2 | 4 |
| 8 | thinnest pencil of 3 | 17 |
| 9 | thickest pencil of 3 | 14 |
| 10 | taller teddy of 2 | 3 |
| 11 | tallest teddy of 3 | 7 |
| 12 | shortest teddy of 3 | 16 |
| 13 | lower kite of 2 | 6 |
| 14 | highest kite of 3 | 2 |
| 15 | lowest kite of 3 | 9 |
| 16 | heavier box of 2 | 6 |
| 17 | heaviest box of 3 | 4 |
| 18 | lightest box of 3 | 6 |
| 19 | nearly empty of 3 | 2 |
| 20 | nearly full of 3 | 1 |
| 21 | contains more of 2 | 4 |
| 22 | contains most of 3 | 10 |
| 23 | contains least of 3 | 24 |

particular aspect of mathematics. Sometimes mathematical language is different and has particular meanings. This is not the case here. The language of measures becomes more specific and precise but can still follow normal usage. We do not want children to think that this mathematical world, that of comparative language, is a new and different one.

The superlative also seems to present problems, more generally, 'Biggest' is easy, highest, heaviest and lightest are not too hard but thinnest and thickest are quite difficult. Again, this probably reflects how much these words are normally used. Overall, however, these results suggest that we can be reasonably sure that many children can deal confidently with comparative language. A proviso we suggest is that they need to work with things they can see and touch. The weight of an object is not easily established by looking at pictures of see-saws. These children also constructed some meanings as the tests proceeded. It is possible to work out a pattern when similar language is being used across a range of measuring terms.

Language about an imaginary situation was employed in the next test to be described, with toys used to model an incident.

### Spatial Language

We wanted to see if children could spontaneously use the positional words: in/inside, under/underneath, next to/beside, on, above/higher up and behind. (One word from these pairs was acceptable and to avoid repetition we shall use the first word of each pair to represent either in this account.) We wanted the children to say the words themselves where possible and not just to recognize them. To this end we set up a story. A mother sheep had a naughty lamb who was always hiding. These toys and a box were in front of the children. The mother sheep faced the children and the lamb was behind her. The children had to help the mother to find her lamb by telling her where it was. After pointing a bit, children soon got the idea that the sheep could not see the lamb and that they must speak to her. Of course we could not ensure that children did not know words because they did not use them. For example, above (or higher up) is heard less often than 'in' or 'on' and as we had expected this caused the most difficulties. We therefore had a fall back position. If children 'failed' to use the word or words we were looking for we asked them to put or hold the lamb in the appropriate position using the box again. That is, we said 'put the lamb behind the box' using whichever words the children had not supplied.

The results were as follows:

- Seven children used all six positional words spontaneously.
- Seventeen children did not use 'above' but were able to respond correctly in the second test.
- Nine children did not use 'next to' or 'above' but were able to respond correctly in the second test.
- Four children did not use 'above' or 'behind' but were able to respond correctly in the second test.
- Three children did not use 'next to', 'above' or 'behind' but were able to respond correctly in the second test.
- Three children did not use 'under' or 'above' but were able to respond correctly in the second test.
- Four children did not use the following words:
  (a) 'under', 'next to', 'on', 'above',
  (b) 'under', 'next to', 'above', 'behind',
  (c) 'next to', 'above', 'behind',
  (d) 'next to', 'on', 'above',
  but all of them could respond correctly in the second test.

Only three children failed to attain 100 per cent of either use or recognition of a positional word and in each case it was 'above' which foiled them. Given the story situation, the children gave an impressive demonstration of their knowledge of spatial language.

### *Is There Any Relationship Between the Durham Project, Classroom Practice and the Constructivist Theme of this Book?*

As we freely admit, and shall discuss later, teachers do not have the time or opportunity to talk and interact with individual children for hours at a time. However, the Durham Project may have points of interest for teaching. Where teachers get the chance to talk with individuals or groups, which are seized upon where possible, our experience may be helpful. We learned a lot about how children respond eagerly to an interested adult. Their attention span was remarkably long. Clearly, we were not teaching but, as we have hinted, being asked questions or set problems encourages children to think. They were also given time to do so. They needed to have some knowledge about the problems they were being set but some of them were likely to have been presented in a new form. This meant that the children were constructing new slants on existing concepts.

Many of our tests could be termed as constructivist in nature. We have already mentioned the story format of the test for spatial language. Throughout we used toy panda who could be told the answers (especially as he was not very clever and needed help from the children). Our intention was to make the situation one with which children were familiar by using many toys that they would have at home or in the nursery. In effect we were negotiating with each child a series of incidents where the props and the stories put the tests into a familiar context.

Sorting was one context children were very familiar with. This related to Attainment Target 5 of Mathematics 5–16 (Data Handling), where children are required to be able to sort using consistent criteria. The request to sort a collection of tiny sorting toys — cars, lorries, cats, dogs, boats — of different colours and sizes threw none of the children. Sorting is done in nurseries but our experience as parents indicated that young children classify all the time before coming to school. They classify in order to learn language and when they play they sort and classify their toys using very fine distinctions. We were not surprised, therefore, that all the children in the study could sort and explain their reasons for their choices. The majority sorted the toys by type though a few used colour. Some did both, usually starting with type and then making sub-sets of colour. Often children who sorted by type added location as a criterion — the horses in the field, the boats in the water and so on. Two children would only sort the toys which would stand up. If we had been teaching we could have developed this idea profitably. That is, an important notion in data handling is to show that a relationship does not exist. 'These toys stand up but those do not' would have been an extension of the children's thinking worth promoting.

We suggest that children, almost without exception, can sort objects and say why or show why they have used their criteria. Perhaps the lesson we draw is that criteria should be extended. Colour, size and shape may be too limiting when there are so many variables which could be employed, such as texture, type, use, material and so on, and as we have indicated above, the introduction of the negative aspect. We did not provide a reason for the sorting we asked the children to do as we wanted an open ended response. However, in the classroom purposes might be easy to think of.

It may be appropriate to explain here why the Durham Project did not explore 'pre-number' activities. (Sorting was not regarded as such an activity but as early data handling.) This was because we have become convinced that number concepts are developed by counting objects of all kinds in a variety of ways and not by sorting, ordering and matching. That is, we question the value of these activities when they are deployed by drawing lines between drawings of identical objects or matching pairs or by colouring 'sets' of pictures or drawing circles round pictures of identical objects. Drawing lines to 'match' identical objects is expected to teach children one:one correspondence. But does it do so? It seems far more likely that children construct early number concepts by pointing, touching or moving objects, counting as they do so. Where there are no more objects to count, then the idea of the cardinal number presents itself immediately. Life gets more complicated when objects are in a pile or a circle or you have to count so many from a larger set. But most of the children in our study could do all this and the sorts of pre-number activities which are being questioned normally appear in school in mathematics schemes, not in the nursery or at home.

In a comprehensive review of available research Young-Loveridge (1987) examines early mathematical instruction and questions whether it needs to be delayed until 'more general cognitive abilities' have appeared' (*ibid.*). In New Zealand (her country) children entering school have to wait a year before exploring number concepts although read-ing instruction begins at once. She argues that matching, ordering, sorting, comparing and classifying (although useful in other respects) are not necessary pre-requisites for being able to deal with number (counting, cardinality, operations, etc.). The reason for the prevalence of pre-number activities stems from Piagetian views about number being a part of a 'single system' so that children are not thought to be able to deal with number until logical thinking has developed. Other cogni-tive psychologists regard number as a 'relatively different cognitive do-main'. Reviewing the available evidence (to which the Durham Project adds weight) Young-Loveridge concludes that there is no evidence what-soever that teaching number too early will be harmful and a great deal which shows that children can and do succeed in mathematical tasks even when they fail Piagetian tasks.

Similarly, but from a different perspective, Womack (1993) ques-tions the 'accepted wisdom of sorting, ordering and matching in order to teach simple number to infants' (*ibid.*). He observed teachers in remote African schools who did not have training or materials but taught children counting, addition and subtraction using sticks, pebbles and the children themselves. We suggest, therefore, that early number should be an oral activity which does not need pre-number activities to be successful. Notation, including symbols, must be introduced in due course but children need not be held back because their motor skills are less advanced than their mathematical attainment.

## How Do Children Learn Before Coming to School?

There have been some studies of children learning at home. For exam-ple, Wells' (1978) extensive studies in Exeter recorded home language and then followed children into school. Tizard and Hughes (1984) moni-tored the experiences of 30 children at home and in nursery school. Hughes (1989) also studied language in the homes of young children. Dunn (1989) looked at the family as an educational environment for young children. The general conclusions drawn from these studies is of the home as a powerful learning environment particularly for language development. The mathematical studies which we have discussed cause us to draw the same conclusions with the added advantage in the Durham Project of a period in nursery education. Of course the home experiences of some children will be different from others whose home life prepares them better for school. If certain school-like experiences are lacking (or at least not apparent) teachers provide them, especially in the nursery. We might, however, consider a project in New Zealand which investigated pupils who were high achievers in mathematics but of low socio-economic status. It found that socio-economic status was less important to high achievement in school than home exposure to a wide range of experience involving numbers including 'baking and shopping, Snakes and Ladders, Strip Jack Naked, Poker, Monopoly, Bingo and dominoes' (Young-Loveridge, 1989).

It is possible to hazard a guess that mathematical conversations may occur in homes even where, for example, parents do not read or write a good deal so children are less generally literate. The ability of so many children to use spatial language in the Durham study is not so surprising when we consider how often these words occur in ordinary talk. 'Just get my my glasses for me pet, I left them on the telly in the front room'. Parents implicitly adopt a constructivist stance when they count fingers or toes, sing number rhymes or play cards with their children. These situations will not provide a progression through mathematics learning in an ordered way, as for example most commercial mathematics schemes do. Number, shape, space, measures, probability will not be separated out, but, as pointed out in chapter 2, mathematical facts and concepts are inter-related. When pre-schoolers meet mathematics at home or in the nursery they are already beginning to learn some 'principles, rules and meanings' (chapter 2) of the subject in a social context. Thus children will become (all too) familiar with 'You have grown. You are taller than Billy now and he's nearly five.' Learning acquired painlessly (but not without being tested against experience) is not superficial and becomes part of children's mental maps. Tizard and Hughes (1984) refer to periods of 'intellectual search' which children engaged in at home. These were conversations children had with adults, about events which interested them, where the child struggled to fit new information into current structures. The adult's role included information but was also characterized by interest and attention to what the child was trying to express. These sorts of conversations were not found even in nursery schools in this research, which, for a number of reasons is not very surprising.

### School Learning

Although children have a propensity to learn and many do so easily at home it would be foolish to underestimate the task teachers have. It could be and has been argued (Tizard and Hughes, *ibid.*) that teachers should learn from parents. This is to underrate the difference between schools and homes. Teachers have to deal with 30 or so children at once not one at a time. Parents also have the great advantage of knowing their children's history, the family, the likely events, what interests children, their moods; in fact a great deal (though not all, as parents would be the first to admit) about them. Teachers do not know all this nor do they pretend to. They have experience of many children in many classes but that very experience warns them about what they do not know. So teachers' constructivism has to be adaptive to classroom situations and a great many individual differences.

Furthermore, unlike parents, teachers have a specific agenda for the content of their teaching. They have a curriculum to implement and always have had even before the advent of the National Curriculum. Parents can and perhaps should be wide ranging in the experiences which they introduce. Teachers are more restricted. Their job is to introduce socially valued knowledge of a particular sort. This includes values and attitudes but curriculum content is prescribed. Enabling children to learn in school, taking up a constructivist stance, may well be harder than enabling them to learn at home. To a certain extent we cannot follow where children lead if we consider the differences of interests and attainment between 30 or so children across ten subjects. The skill of teachers is to balance the autonomy of each learner against the directions which the curriculum must take. Teachers have to interest children in their agendas while enabling children to contribute and use what they already know. (This may include the 'differentiation by outcome' approach as discussed in chapter 2.) We have attempted, in several previous chapters, to make suggestions which enable children to construct their mathematics with the teacher. We should emphasize here that children constructing mathematics is not the same as expecting children to do this on their own. The role of the teacher and her teaching is crucial.

Leaving the Durham Project, another interesting scheme is described by Fenema, Carpenter and Peterson (1989). This involved what was called 'Cognitively Guided Instruction'. The major tenets of CGI are:

(1)   Instruction must be based on what each learner knows.
(2)   Instruction should take into consideration how children's mathematical ideas develop naturally, and
(3)   Children must be mentally active as they learn mathematics (*ibid.*).

The techniques used by the teachers involved in this project do not seem much more than common sense to a British audience. They included the sorts of story formats we have put in chapter 3. Teachers also seized opportunities to pose problems about addition and subtraction (which were the focus of the study) taking a few minutes to use, for example, children who took packed lunch, went home or had school dinners to ask questions. We have often observed these sorts of things in British classrooms where teachers also used the American ploy of often asking children how they arrived at their answers and if anyone else could suggest another way. The American teachers were also aware of the different kinds of addition and subtraction problems there are which are served by the same symbols and that a correct answer, without some probing into how it was arrived at, may not be evidence of understanding.

An important point to consider about this research is, however, that children's progress was dependent on the teacher's knowledge of the mathematics involved, her techniques and her knowledge of how children think about mathematics. So far in this chapter we have looked at mathematics for younger children although we believe that the principles, even if applied rather differently, apply to older primary pupils. Again, it may be useful to teachers if we look at how children and adults learn and use mathematics outside school.

## Real Mathematics?

In this discussion we shall draw extensively on a recent summary of 'street mathematics' written by Nunes, Schlieman and Carraher (1993). Street mathematics is the term these authors use for mathematics employed in everyday life, often by adults and children with little or no formal schooling. Research in this area, therefore, is often carried out in countries where compulsory schooling is brief and of poor quality for poorer sections of the community. Such disadvantage is unfortunate but it does provide opportunities for investigations into informal mathematics use and comparisons with school mathematics.

Nunes *et al.* (*ibid.*) have been working in Brazil for a decade. They have looked at the differences between children's success in oral and written problems, where they often fail the latter because they are confused by trying to apply procedures learned in school instead of thinking about the problem. They have also looked at how unschooled fishermen and carpenters invent and use complex mathematical skills in their daily lives. It is not possible here to summarize a wealth of research but it may be useful here to look at some points of interest which are related to the view we have taken about school learning.

In the first place we must ask if anything can be learned from street mathematics which is applicable to schools. It could be argued that unlike school mathematics, street mathematics is specific to a particular situation and is therefore not able to be extended, transferred or generalized. If that were wholly the case street mathematicians would not be able to solve problems which were not found in their experience. However Nunes *et al.* (*ibid.*) found many instances where experience was able to be adjusted by use of imaginary and different situations. For example, fishermen who used ratio to calculate profit from their catches could extend this skill to an imaginary weight (suggested to them to be the case in another part of the country) to solve problems which were clearly not found in their particular situation. Nunes *et al.* (*ibid.*) also report a study by Dias (1988) where it was made clear to children that, in order to solve certain problems, experience had to be amended 'by inducing children to create a *mental world* (our emphasis) that they temporarily consider in their reasoning'. This notion has resonance with our argument that mathematics in the classroom does not have to be 'real' in the sense of, for example, calculating the amount of drink needed for a party which will actually take place. Reality can be a mental construct in the classroom, we have suggested, which is brought about by social agreement and interaction between children and their teachers.

Nunes *et al.* (*ibid.*) indicate that young children have problems with the concept of a unit of measurement. They may count objects correctly but do not easily grasp that for example, ten 2p coins has a different value from ten 20p coins. This will come as no surprise to teachers. Young street traders must, of course, understand the notion of a unit very quickly. They do so even if they are illiterate but are familiar with a money economy. Again this is not surprising but it does draw attention to the necessity, in school, of using units of measurement. It is a very different thing to measure a line in a book from measuring the length of a worm or a gerbil. Measurement requires these real activities, although the reason for the measurement of money, distance, weight, area and so on can be a construct which makes sense to children. Measuring for a purpose will almost always give results which are not tidy, that is not 3cm but a bit more or a bit less. This sort of result enables children to understand that measurement is never exact because it depends on the size of the unit selected which can be infinitely large or small (but needs to be appropriate — not centimetres for the hall). Furthermore, it is the use of any unit, be it in coins, minutes, metres, cupfulls or whatever which enables children to estimate. A fisherman can estimate the weight (and value) of his catch and a quantity surveyor the cost of a building because of their extensive experience. Neither children nor adults can estimate without experience.

When Nunes *et al.* (*ibid.*) consider the implications of their research for teachers they draw attention to the concept of 'realistic mathematics education' which they say is most developed in the Freudenthal Institute in Utrecht.

> Realistic mathematics education involves posing to pupils in the classroom problems that require the consideration of empirical constants as well as social and logical rules that apply outside school. In this conception, solving a problem involves making decisions about how to proceed in imagined situations (*ibid.*).

They agree that it is hard to think of good problems to work on in classrooms. Some problems or situations they suggest may fly in the face of logic too much. For example, Nunes *et al.* (*ibid.*) quote Gravemeijer (1990) saying that the following problem becomes a joke. 'There were ten birds in a tree, two were killed by gunshot. How many were left?'

We can agree with Nunes *et al.* (*ibid.*) that the first problem shown below makes more sense that the second:

A problem from realistic mathematic education.
Tonight 81 parents will visit school. At each table 6 parents can
    be seated
How many tables will we need?

An unrealistic problem about time.

John ate 8 Big Macs. It takes 25 minutes to eat a Big Mac. How long did it take him to eat them all?

We drew attention above to the suggestion that 'reality' can be a mental construct in the classroom. A good deal of what we have discussed in this book relates to such mental constructs. We do not necessarily agree with the idea of 'realistic mathematics education' depending on what interpretation is put on 'empirical constants as well as social and logical rules that apply outside school'. As we have made clear we do not believe that mathematical situations in the classroom need to be 'real' in the sense that they could actually occur. An important part of anyone's life as well as events which happen are those which might happen and those which are unlikely or impossible. We refer, of course, to the imagination, to fantasy and to stories. Imagination, fantasy and story are part of social and cultural experience. We were not indulging in whimsy when we asked children to talk with a panda in the Durham Project, nor when we encouraged participation in dramatic play, as in chapter 3. For instance, the children were as aware as we were that toy pandas do not talk or listen. We were drawing on those parts of their experiences which are different from the empirical but which are part of reality.

To some extent a great deal of school learning seems to have little connection with the world outside school. We no longer ask children to solve odd problems about how long it takes x workmen to dig y ditches at z rate. But we do ask them very often to take on trust, that what we are teaching is worth while. As deferred gratification — 'it (may) help you get a good job' — is rather remote, it may well be more productive to construct situations in school, where what we are doing in mathematics makes sense in that situation and gives point to activities. It is possible that doing so may be more productive, rather than less so, to children understanding that mathematics has uses and applications outside of school.

The need to construct a 'mental world' in which mathematics comes alive and is necessary is evident if they are to use and apply what they know or learn of mathematics by using it. Looking rather more broadly at mental worlds we can consider topics or projects. It has been argued (Palmer and Pettitt, 1993) that no subject should be included in a topic unless it has a sensible and justifiable place in that topic. Nevertheless, a powerful reason for doing topics in the primary school is that, when done well, the whole topic is a mental construct where learning, including learning mathematics, becomes less neat and tidy but opens up the rich variety of concepts subjects involve.

Thus, a topic on 'shopping' or 'minibeasts' or 'the environment' to name very few, involves money, measuring or co-ordinates and enables mathematics to be used. Similarly, topics focused on science or history require data handling skills. We are not arguing against the need for mathematics to be done separately; for revision or practice or new learning. Nor do we dispute that children take pleasure in doing pages of sums. Nor do we deny, indeed we advocate, that mathematics can be done for the intrinsic enjoyment of puzzling out its principles. Nevertheless, pages of sums are not necessarily able to be transferred to new situations. That is, each skill may be limited to a particular page and not connected to other modes of presentation. Enjoying mathematics for the pleasure of wrestling with a problem may be the province of too few children. Many more ways forward need to be found to bring the majority of children to think mathematically and some of these may have been suggested in our previous chapters.

### Conclusion

University lecturers, researchers, advisers and even (because of new pressures) head teachers can forget, all too easily, what it is like to be a classroom teacher. Nothing that any of these people (including ourselves) say or do is profitable unless it can be used by teachers in their classrooms. It is classroom teachers who will, if it is possible, raise standards and it is they who will or will not think it possible or profitable to implement some of our proposals. Much of what we suggest comes from our own experience as teachers and from teachers with whom we have worked. We should like to conclude, therefore, not by repeating what we have suggested but by leaving the last word with a teacher. The Durham Project, in its second phase, funded by ESRC, enabled us to observe Reception class teachers in action. They were also kind enough to give us their views on teaching mathematics. The following are excerpts from what one teacher said to us.

On feeling comfortable with mathematics
(After saying that she had always liked mathematics)

> I think infant (teachers) took Cockroft on board much more quickly than anyone else did. And I think that one of the possible reasons is the discipline reason in that a child sat down doing a pile of sums is quiet and the teacher feels in control of the situation. . . . (some teachers can still) get frightened because children are talking to one another. . . .

(on her concept of 'quality time')

> you can't teach everybody at the same level, all of the time . . .
> Your aim isn't to make everybody a professor of mathematics . . .
> (a lower attaining child) has still got to enjoy mathematics at the level she is operating.

On key concepts in mathematics in the Reception class

> I've thought about this for a long time. Number . . . symbols and number and then operations . . . , the language of mathematics.

Shape and pattern, sequencing ordering, measurement to a certain extent but I think they learn a lot of measurement not in school. Children learn to tell the time not in school. And we spend a lot of time doing it. . . .

The National Curriculum is a wonderful check list. The trouble is other things have made AT1 not happen. . . . The problem with AT1 is people don't know how to do it. . . . The best way I've found is to do it with a whole class . . . then set it up and leave it set up while there's still interest there . . . with the slower ones I revisit it and I revisit it with the whole class as well. . . . You are constantly reflecting on what is happening and who is doing what, which you can do with 25 quite easily. . . .

On how children learn

I think it's this small group situation . . . me sat with them with either a game or an activity . . . even if its actually writing sums . . . I would still sit with them, keeping tabs on them and what I need to adjust.

After discussing the difficulty of getting it all in:

Your maths games aren't a Friday activity, that's done when you've finished your work and as an extra. You know why you are doing it and what they are learning from it as long as you adapt it for your learning situation. I look at them and think 'What do I want from this?' . . . I think my most valuable equipment is maths games. . . . you can work with children at different levels to stretch your more able (children) — you have got to think through what you want from it and then know you are going to have W . . . and what can I add for him or for S . . . or whatever.

Direct teaching versus discovery.

I think Plowden was misinterpreted. I think it was right that the child and their needs are first and then you match and that's when somehow, somebody got the message that you don't teach children. I don't know why but it came through.

I don't know why it did, that children must discover for themselves . . . unless you've got a repertoire of certain things you are not going to learn anything. How can I explain what I mean? You have got to teach children something so they can go on and discover . . . you have got to teach them how to learn, and you've got to teach them facts and methods as well and how to do things . . . . . . learning is like an apprenticeship isn't it, you know, we are further on in life so we pass on what we've learnt by showing, speaking, explaining, talking, getting something back, you know this exchange. . . . Lets get AT1 really talked about but how can we do it?

The teacher goes on to discuss the overcrowded curriculum:

I think the only way we can get the core (subjects) right is more time and to explain it more fully to everybody. Because I think we are just being like butterflies flitting from one to the other.

I don't do a lot of recording in maths. The children have got to write sums but day after day of sums and sums isn't teaching a child maths it's simply keeping them out of your hair.

The word progress is very, very misleading as is achievement really. What you see is change. Progress infers that you are going linear forward, achieve suggests a mountain you are going to climb and neither of those tally with learning theories — that you are doing this aren't you; forward and back, forward and back.

There are a lot of things Reception children know that are what I would call roots of the plant, that you can't see, that they don't tell you, but nevertheless is being absorbed, being learnt . . . must have a good strong root system before any leaves are going to shoot on top.

On planning and commercial schemes:

I have used them all (commercial schemes). I can find fault with them all. Nevertheless, yes we need them, to be honest, for a variety of reasons. When you are experienced, when you are supplying, it needs continuity in the schools and some teachers do need them . . . you see the ideas and you know the sequence . . . I haven't done much data handling for a while — we better do it. I'm very much against in this fortnight you do data handling for a while and this fortnight we do shape and in this fortnight you do number and so forth.

On attitude:

Then there is this idea of attitude. That with young children is very important. In fact I think they pick up more than they do with the spoken word. I think they take on board, they know, whether you like maths, whether you are excited by what you are doing . . .

On advice to a student:

Get the basic organization in your classroom so independent learning can go on and that frees you to do what you planned.

On giving a lot of yourself and to some extent exposing yourself to a student and colleagues:

Yes, you've got to be prepared to laugh at yourself and say 'This isn't working, put it away'.

They think I can't sit down with every child and do an investigation. You can't. You can sit down with a big group, you can sit down with a small group. If the group are familiar with it (the investigation) the children will talk about it as well. So actually children will learn something from children as well.

I hope I am being a help (to a student) because I think it really must be an apprenticeship. For too long we have been in our own classrooms with our cupboards locked and I think we have been a very unsharing bunch of people . . . . We have just got to come out and say. But then you have got to be the sort of person that can trip over a banana skin and pick themselves up and laugh and get on with it because it is going to happen when you do that.

Obviously, these very small extracts are taken from a transcript of a conversation. We could have tidied up what was said but we would not presume to do so nor would we have wished to tamper with the thinking of an experienced and excellent teacher. She may not do in her classroom all the things we have suggested, but it is transparent to us that this is what we mean by a constructivist teacher.

# References

AHMED, A. (1987) *Better Mathematics. A Curriculum Development Study*, London: HMSO.

ALEXANDER, R. (1992) *Policy and Practice In Primary Education*, London: Routledge.

ATHEY, C. (1990) *Extending Thought in Young Children*, London: Paul Chapman Publishing Ltd.

AUBREY, C. (1994) 'An investigation of children's knowledge of mathematics at school entry and the knowledge their teachers hold about teaching and learning mathematics, about young learners and mathematical subject knowledge', *British Educational Research Journal*, **Vol. 20**, No. 1.

BAILEY, C. (1984) *Beyond the Present and the Particular*, London: Routledge, p. 54 ff.

BELL, L.A. and DAY, C. (1991) *Managing the Professional Development of Teachers*, Milton Keynes: Open University Press.

BILLINGTON, J. and EVANS, P. (1987) 'Levels of knowing 2. The handshake', *Mathematics Teaching*, **120**.

BOLTON, G. (1979) *Towards a theory of drama in Education*, London: Longman.

BRISSENDEN, T. (1988) *Talking about Mathematics*, Oxford: Blackwell.

BUCKHAM, J. (1994) 'Teachers' understanding of children's drawings', in AUBREY, C. (Ed.) *The Role of Subject Knowledge in the Early Years of Schooling*, London: The Falmer Press.

COURT, E. (1992) 'Researching social influences in the drawings of rural Kenyan children', in THISTLEWOOD, D. *et al.* (Eds) *Drawing Research and Development*, Harlow: Longman.

COX, M.V. (1991) *The Child's Point of View*, Hemel Hempstead: Harvest Wheatsheaf.

DAVIS, A. (1990) 'Logical defects of the TGAT report', *British Journal of Educational Studies*, **XXXVIII**, No. 3.

DAVIS, A. (1993) 'Matching and assessment', *Journal of Curriculum Studies*, **25**, 3.

# References

DAVIS, R.B. (1984) *Learning Mathematics*, London: Croom Helm.

DEARING, RON (1994) *The National Curriculum and its assessment: Final Report*, London: SCAA.

DES (1991) *In-Service Training for the Introduction of the National Curriculum*, HMSO.

DES (1992) *Art in the National Curriculum; Non-Statutory Guidance for Teachers*, Curriculum Council for Wales.

DESFORGES, C. (1989) 'Understanding Learning for Teachers', *Westminster Studies in Education*, **Vol. 12**.

DESFORGES, C. and COCKBURN, A. (1987) *Understanding the Mathematics Teacher*, Lewes: Falmer.

DIENES, Z.P. (1960) *Building up Mathematics*, London: Hutchinson.

DONALDSON, M. (1978) *Children's Minds*, London: Fontana.

DUBERY, F. and WILLATS, J. (1993) *Perspective and other Drawing Systems*, London: Hobart Press Ltd.

DUNN, J. (1989) *The Family as an Educational Environment in the Pre-school Years*, Edinburgh: Scottish Academic Press Ltd.

ERNEST, P. (1986) 'GAMES — A rationale for their use in the teaching of mathematics in school', *Mathematics in School*, **15**, pp. 2–5.

ERNEST, P. (1991) *The Philosophy of Mathematics Education*, London: Falmer.

FENEMA, E., CARPENTER, T.P. and PETERSON, P.L. (1989) 'Learning mathematics with understanding: Cognitively guided instruction', in BROPHY, J. (Ed.) *Advances in Research on Teaching*, **Vol. 1**, London: JAI Press.

GATTEGNO, C. (1958) *From Actions to Operations*, Reading: Cuisenaire and Co. Ltd.

GOLDIN, G.A. (1990) 'Epistemology, constructivism and discovery learning in mathematics', in DAVIS, B.F., MAHER, C.A. and NODDINGS, N. (Eds) *Constructivist Views on the Teaching and Learning of Mathematics*, Virginia: NCTM.

GOLOMB, C. (1992) *The Child's Creation of a Pictorial World*, Berkely, C.A.: University of California Press.

GOULDING, M. (1993) 'Roamin' to music', *Strategies*, **Vol. 3**, No. 3.

HAYLOCK, D. and COCKBURN, A. (1989) *Understanding Early Years Mathematics*, London: Paul Chapman.

HEATHCOTE, D. (1984) *Collected writings on Education and Drama*, London: Hutchinson.

HEWTON, A. (1988) *School Focused Staff Development*, London: Falmer Press.

HUGHES, M. (1989) 'The child as a learner: The contrasting view of developmental psychology and early education', in DESFORGES, C.

(Ed.) *Early Childhood Education*, Edinburgh: Scottish Academic Press Ltd.

JOHNSON, D. (Ed.) (1989) *Children's Mathematical Frameworks 8–13*, Windsor: NFER-Nelson.

KIRKBY, D. (1983) *Number Activity in the Classroom*, Sheffield: Eigen Publications.

McNAMARA, D. (1994) *Classroom Pedagogy and Primary Practice*, London: Routledge.

MATTHEWS, J. (1988) 'The young child's early representation in drawing', in BLENKIN, G.M. and KELLY, A.V. (Eds) *Early Childhood Education: A Developmental Curriculum*, London: Paul Chapman.

MATTHEWS, J. (1991) 'How children map 3D volumes and scenes on flat surfaces', in JONES, L. (Ed.) *Teaching Mathematics and Art*, Cheltenham: Stanley Thornes Publishing Ltd.

MILLWARD, P. (1988) 'Language and Drama', Unpublished Ph.D. thesis, University of Durham, England.

NUNES, T., SCHIELMANN, A. and CARREHER, D. (1993) *Street Mathematics and School Mathematics*, Cambridge: Cambridge University Press.

OFSTED (1993) *Curriculum Organisation and Classroom Practice in Primary Schools*, DFE Publications Centre.

PALEY, V.G. (1981) *Wally's stories*, London: Harvard University Press.

PALMER, J. and PETTITT, D. (1993) *Topic Work in the Early Years*, London: Routledge.

POLYA, G. (1945) *How to Solve it*, Princeton, New Jersey: Princeton University Press.

SCHOENFELD, A. (1988) 'Research on Problem Solving', in *Problem Solving — A World View, The Proceedings of the Problem Solving Theme Group, 5th International Congress of Mathematics Education, Adelaide*, The Shell Centre for Mathematics Education, University of Nottingham.

SINCLAIR, J. and COULTHARD, R. (1975) *Towards an Analysis of Discourse*, London: Oxford University Press.

SKEMP, R. (1989) *Mathematics in the Primary School*, London: Routledge.

SMITH, N.R. (1983) *Experience and Art: Teaching Children to Paint*, New York: Teachers' College Press.

SMITH, N.R. (1992) 'The development of the aesthetic in children's drawings', in THISTLEWOOD, D. *et al.* (Eds) *Drawing Research and Development*, Harlow: Longman.

STEFFE, L.P. and WIEGEL, H.G. (1992) 'On reforming practice in mathematical education', *Educational Studies in Mathematics*, **23**, pp. 445–65.

TAYLOR, R. (1986) *Educating for Art*, Harlow: Longman.

## References

THOMPSON, I. (1993) 'Thirteen ways to solve a problem', *Mathematics Teaching*, **144**.

THORNTON, C. (1989) *Arithmetic Teacher*, **Vol. 36,** 8, pp. 8–11.

TIZARD, B. and HUGHES, M. (1984) *Young Children Learning: Talking and Thinking at Home or in School*, London: Fontana.

TOLKIEN, J. (1964) *Tree and Leaf*, London: Unwin.

VARKALIS, A. (1992) 'Bilingualism and bi-cultural approaches to art and design', *Journal of Art and Design Education*, **Vol. 11,** No. 2.

VON GLASERSFELD, E. (1987) 'Learning as a constructive activity', in JANVIER, C. (Ed.) *Problems of Representation in Teaching and Learning of Mathematics*, Hillsdale NJ: Erlbaum.

WALTER, M. and BROWN, S. (1969) 'What if not?', *Mathematics Teaching*, **No. 46**.

WELLS, G.C. (1978) 'Talking with children: The complementary roles of parents and teachers', *English in Education*, **12**, pp. 15–38.

WERNER, H. and KAPLAN, B. (1963) *Symbol Formation*, New York: John Wiley and Sons.

WILLATS, J. (1985) 'Drawing systems revisited: The role of denotation systems in children's figure drawing', in FREEMAN, N. and COX, M.V. (Eds) *Visual Order*, New York: Cambridge University Press.

WILLATS, J. (1992) 'What is the matter with Mary Jane's drawing?', in THISTLEWOOD, D. *et al.* (Eds) *Drawing Research and Development*, Harlow: Longman.

WILSON, B. (1992) 'Primitivism, the avant-garde and the art of little children', in THISTLEWOOD, D. *et al.* (Eds) *Drawing Research and Development*, Harlow: Longman.

WILSON, B., HURWITZ, A. and WILSON, M. (1987) *Teaching Drawing from Art*, Worcester, MA: Davis Publications Inc.

WILSON, B. and LIGTVOET (1992) 'Across time and cultures: Stylistic change in the drawings of Dutch children', in THISTLEWOOD, D. *et al.* (Eds) *Drawing Research and Development*, Harlow: Longman.

WILSON, B. and WILSON, M. (1980) 'The Use of Conventional Configurations, Images and Themes in the Narrative Drawings of American Children', in *Art and Cultural Diversity INSEA 23rd World Congress*, Sydney: Holt Rinehart and Winston.

WOLF, D. (1989) 'Artistic learning as conversation', in HARGREAVES, D.J. (Ed.) *Children and the Arts*, Buckingham: Open University Press.

WOLF, D. *et al.* (1988) 'Beyond A, B and C: A broader and deeper view of literacy', in PELLEGRINI, A.D., *The Psychological Bases for Early Education*, Chichester: John Wiley and Sons.

WOLF, D. and PERRY, M.D. (1988) 'From endpoint to repertoire, some new conclusions about drawing development', *Journal of Aesthetic Development*, **Vol. 22**, 1.

WOMACK, D. (1993) 'Game, set and match', TES, 8 October, 1993.

YOUNG-LOVERIDGE, J.M. (1987) 'Learning mathematics', *British Journal of Educational Psychology*, **5**, pp. 155–67.

YOUNG-LOVERIDGE, J.M. (1989) 'The relationship between children's home experiences and their mathematical skills on entry to school', *Early Child Development and Care*, **Vol. 43**, pp. 43–59.

# Notes on Contributors

*Editors*

**Andrew Davis** is Director of the PGCE Primary Course at Durham University and Lecturer in Early Years and Mathematics. He contributes to INSET and the MA programme in Mathematics Education. Previously a primary teacher for many years, he then moved to Homerton College, Cambridge to teach Philosophy of Education. Research interests include philosophical psychology of mathematics learning, and assessment. Publications include several related academic papers, together with computer software, and various curriculum articles in magazines such as Junior Education and Infant Projects.

**Deirdre Pettitt** lectures in the School of Education at the University of Durham. She moved from infant teaching into higher education at the University of East Anglia, where she directed the Early Years teacher education course (1985 to 1987). Her major research interest is Early Years. Since 1990 she has worked with Carol Aubrey on the investigation of informal mathematical knowledge children bring to school. Her publications include (with Joy Palmer) *Topic Work in the Early Years* — *4–8* (1993, London, Routledge), and chapters on history and writing in *The Role of Subject Knowledge in the Early Years of Schooling*, edited by Carol Aubrey (1994, Falmer Press).

*Other Writers*

**Jennifer Buckham** is an artist and art-educator and has had experience of teaching all age groups of children. She taught for thirteen years in both primary and secondary schools in Nairobi and London before moving into higher education. She worked as a lecturer at Kingston Polytechnic and the University of Exeter before joining the School of Education in Durham. Her main area of research is concerned with children's drawing development and repertoire. She has built up an extensive collection and record of children's work in both Kenyan and British contexts and has a particular interest in individual case studies. She contributed to *The Role of Subject Knowledge in the Early Years of Schooling*, edited by Carol Aubrey (1994, Falmer Press).

**Maria Goulding** lectures in Mathematics Education at Durham University. She has worked in teacher education for ten years, having previously taught in inner city schools in Liverpool. She has been involved in the professional preparation of primary and secondary teachers of mathematics and has worked extensively in school-based In-Service Education. Her research interests include the use of calculators and computers, and gender issues. She has written in both these areas. Several of her publications appear in journals of the Association of Teachers of Mathematics, of which she is the Durham Branch Secretary.

**Peter Millward** directs the BA(Ed) Course at Durham University. He lectures in Language and Drama for Initial Teacher Education, INSET, the MA programme and supervises higher degree work. His research interests are child language and drama: *Language of Drama* (doctoral thesis, 1988), *Drama as a Well-made Play* (Language Arts, 1990), *Children Talking About Poetry* (with Linda Thompson, 1991), and *The Role of Subject Knowledge in the Early Years of Schooling*, edited by Carol Aubrey (1994, Falmer Press).

**Brian Woodhouse** lectures in Education at the University of Durham and has taught mathematics from university degree level to Key Stage 1. He has also extensive experience in In-service teaching and contributes to the MA programme. He has a particular interest in both mathematical and educational aspects of concepts in probability and statistics.

# Index

# Index